Lewis L. [from old catalog] Evarts

Has Spiritualism Any Foundation in the Bible?

Lewis L. [from old catalog] Evarts

Has Spiritualism Any Foundation in the Bible?

ISBN/EAN: 9783337172275

Printed in Europe, USA, Canada, Australia, Japan

Cover: Foto ©Lupo / pixelio.de

More available books at **www.hansebooks.com**

Has Spiritualism Any Foundation in the Bible?

BY

L. L. EVARTS.

PRICE 25 CENTS.

PREFACE.

This little book is sent forth on its mission among men, by the author, with the firm conviction that it is a necessity—as "Modern Spiritualism," with all its soul-inspiring truths, has to suffer so much misrepresentation at the hands of those who know nothing of the sublime teachings of this heaven-horn philosophy—to educate the people from a Bible standpoint.

No doubt a great many, even among the thoughtful, will be surprised at the statement that the intervention of angels in human affairs is a very conspicuous element in the sacred books, and that hardly a great event is recorded there, in which they have not been prominent actors. As the question has been so often asked, "What saith the Scriptures in regard to spiritualism," the author has gone to considerable trouble in order to answer the above question, or rather, to put facts in such shape that the Scriptures may answer for themselves, and this, I think, has been so well done, that the reader must see, at least, the wonderful affinity between Bible spiritualism and that which is known as "Modern Spiritualism."

This little book is also intended to teach that a materializing seance does not contain all there is in spiritualism, as some would-be exposers would have the public believe, and indeed, judging from the utterences of some of our religious leaders, we are forced to the conclusion that they, too, entertain the same crude idea. Then there are others who—strange to say, have never investigated in order to find out what spiritualism really is—very readily admit the facts, but they attribute all to his "Satanic Majesty." If such can lay aside their prejudice and give this book an impartial reading, carefully comparing the Scriptures therein referred to, I think they would come to the conclusion that spiritualism must be a mighty uncomfortable place for such a notable personage. As the reader peruses the pages of this book he will find that the greatest men of the present day are avowed Spiritualists, and all over the world millions are rejoicing in the benign influences of "Modern Spiritualism." They believe in the continued love and helpfulness of the departed; they have certainly revived the ancient faith, and boldly assert what every personage of the New, and every prophet of the Old Testament would assert, that heaven is within speaking distance, and that the constant companionship of angels is one of the inalienable rights of aspiring souls.

If Christians had thoroughly believed the Bible and accepted its revelations in this regard, it may be that "Modern Spiritualism" would never have been born. Now it must be stated that the author lays no claim to any phase of mediumship; he is but an humble student of the truth, and as this little book is sent out in the interest of the truth, free from all spirit of controversy, he has no fears as to the ultimate results, whatever may be the opinion of bigots who are wise in their own conceit of the subject of which this book treats. And I am sure that no fair-minded, no philosophic thinker, will dream of treating it with derision or contempt.

JOHN FORTUNE.

HAS SPIRITUALISM ANY FOUNDATION IN THE BIBLE ?

<hr style="width:20%">

IS Spiritualism true? is a question that at the present time, as never before, is agitating the minds of the masses (There being about ten million adherents in the U. S.) and, as Spiritualism finds its worst opposition in those who are, or at least claim to be believers in the Bible, this little book is sent forth in the hope that it may give a satisfactory answer to the above question from a Bible standpoint. Webster defines Spiritualism as "A belief in the frequent communication of intelligences from the world of spirits by means of physical phenomena, commonly manifested through persons of special susceptibility, called mediums." Before proceeding further we wish to settle a question that is often asked by our "orthodox friends," that is, is there no distinction between an angel and a spirit? To make it appear that the Bible ignores spirit return, the Church draws a line of distinction between the two. Psalms 104:4 reads : "Who maketh his angels spirits, his ministers a flaming fire." The angel that John saw on the Isle of Patmos was the spirit of one of the prophets. "And I, John, saw these things and heard them. And when I had heard and seen, I fell down to worship before the feet of the angel which showed me these things : Then saith he unto me, See thou do it not for I am thy fellow-servant, and of thy brethren, the prophets." —a human spirit.—Rev 22:8:9. Angels are ministering spirits.

"But unto which of the angels saith he at any time, Sit on my right hand, until I make thine enemies thy foot stool? Are they not all ministering spirits sent forth to minister for those who shall be heirs of salvation"—Heb. 1:13:14. In Gen. 3:8, a being called "the Lord God." Elohim walks through the garden, and talks with Adam and Eve. In Verses 21 to 24 this same being makes clothing out of skins for them, and drives them from the garden. Gen. 12:1 to 7—the Lord speaks unto Abraham, also appears unto him. Acts 7:2:6 says: "The Lord of glory appeared unto our father Abraham and called him out to sojourn in a strange land." In Gen. 17:1, This same spirit (God is a spirit) appeared to Abraham again and said: "I am Almighty God." He afterwards spoke unto Moses, and told him he had appeared unto Abraham as "Almighty God," but his real name, which he kept from Abraham, was Jehovah.—Exod. 6:2:3. Moses, Aaron, Nadab, Abihu, and seventy of the elders of Israel—74 persons—saw God.—Exod. 24:9 to 11. We ask our orthodox friends, do you believe these persons ever saw, and talked with God? The answer comes, yes, I believe it because the Bible says so. We now ask our friend to turn to John 1:18 which reads: "No man hath seen God at any time." I John 4: 12 reads the same, "No man hath seen God at any time." I Tim. 6:16 reads: "Whom no man hath seen, nor can see." John 5: 37 reads: "Ye have neither heard his voice at any time nor seen his shape." I Tim. 1:17 and Col. 1:15 declares that God is invisible. Exod. 33:20, God tells Moses "No man shall see me and live."

We again ask our friend, do you believe the statement that "No man hath seen God at any time?" and he will answer us by saying that we are an infidel, or sceptic, and the pulpit will hurl its anathemas at us for daring to question "God's Holy Word." Since but one of these statements can be true, I choose to believe the latter; our orthodox friends may believe both.

The Bible says: "Come now let us reason together." I want to say, I cannot believe that God was ever seen by any mortal, not so much because the Bible says so, but because I can only conceive of God as being omnipresent, and as such he can only be seen as he is revealed to us in His works. In Abraham's time, any spirit that communicated or gave any manifestations, whether they were one or more, were called "The Lord." In Genesis, 18th chapter, "the Lord" appears to Abraham. He is called "the Lord" eight times; "my Lord" once; "three men" once; and "the men" once. The manifestations were wonderful. The first Abraham knew the Lord appeared unto him. He looked up "and lo! three men stood by him." He did not see them come to him, they appeared, as Moses and Elias appeared to Jesus, and as Jesus "appeared to two of them as they walked, and went into the country." They were materializations that could be handled, and they had their feet washed.—Verse 4.

They also ate "a square meal," consisting of bread, veal, cake, butter, and milk.—Verses 6 to 8. It is absurd to suppose that a spirit could partake of such coarse material food, or have their feet washed, but there is nothing mysterious about it, if we admit they were clothed in material bodies. After they had their dinner, they revealed to Abram the impending doom of Sodom. Verses 20 and 21 read : "And the Lord said, Because the cry of Sodom and Gomorrah is great, and because their sin is very grievous, I will go down now, and see whether they have done altogether according to the cry of it, and if not, I will know." Gen. 11:5 reads : "And the Lord came down to see the city and the tower, which the children of men builded." Candidly now, do you think this could be said of an omnipresent, omniscient God? I cannot think so. Gen. 19:1 says that two angels came to Abraham's brother Lot in Sodom.

These two persons are called angels twice, Verses 1 and 15; they are called men six times, Verses 5, 8, 10, 11, 12, and 16; they are "sent of the Lord" three times, Verses 13, 14 and 16; and they are called "my Lord" once, Verse 18. These also partook of material food, Verse 3. Gen. 32:24 to 32, Jacob wrestles with one of these heavenly visitants. Verse 24 says it was a man. In Verse 30 Jacob concludes that he has really had a tussle with God himself. "And Jacob called the name of the place Peniel, for I have seen God face to face, and my life is preserved." In Exodus 3:2 to 6, the angel of the Lord appears to Moses "in the burning bush." This spirit, in Verse 2, is called "the angel of the Lord." In Verse 4, both Lord and God. Verse 6 says : Moses was afraid to look upon God. In Judges, 13th Chapter, 3 to 22, a spirit being appeared first to the wife of Manoah, the Danite, and then to Manoah. This appearance is called an angel of the Lord 9 times, in Verses 3, 13, 15, 16, 17, 18, 20 and 21; an angel once, Verse 19; a man 3 times, Verse 10 and 11; a man of God twice, Verses 6 to 8; Angel of God once, Verse 9.

And finally Manoah believes it to have been God himself, for in Verse 22, "Manoah said unto his wife, We shall surely die, because we have seen God." In the 28th chapter of I Samuel, 13th verse, the spirit of Samuel comes to Saul through the woman of En-dor. In answer to Saul's words : "Be not afraid for what sawest thou?" the woman said unto Saul, "I saw gods ascending out of the earth." I have tried thus far to show how these heavenly visitants were taken for, or else were called gods. Had I lived in Abraham's time, no doubt, I too, would have taken these heavenly visitants for gods, if I know as little of spirit return as he did. Aaron was one of the 74 persons who saw God, (Exodus 24:9 to 11), and yet but a little time after we find him making a golden calf for he and the people to worship—Exodus 32:1 to 5. Had I really seen God, as Aaron is said to have seen him, I hardly think that I would have wandered away from Him so quick and worshipped a god of gold which my own hand had fashioned, but the circumstance only shows how common a thing it was for these so-called gods to appear unto men. That these influences called the Lord are not always the same individuality is proved by comparing II Sam. 24:1 with I Chron. 21:1. Both texts teach that David was moved by a spirit influence, but while the former says it was the Lord moved David to number Israel, the latter leaves the Lord out, and says that it was Satan that provoked David to number Israel. It is evident that the Lords and Satans of Old Testament times were simply spirits, nothing more, nor nothing less. "No man hath seen God at any time (I John 4:12 and John 1:18). Who then was the spirit being who came to Abram and said: "I am Almighty God." We believe him to have been a very ancient spirit who was interested in the welfare of the Jewish nation. In Judges 1:19 we read, "And the Lord was with Judah and he drave out the inhabitants of the mountain, but he could not drive out the inhabitants of the valley because they had chariots of iron." I believe, my dear orthodox friends, that the Ruler of this Universe could have driven out the inhabitants of the valley, as well as those of the mountain. If he could not, then he is not Almighty God.

But we will come now more direct to the subject. Is Spiritualism true? As Spiritualism is simply a belief in spirit return, let us ask, is spirit return true? We answer yes, and to take spirit return out of the Bible, you would have nothing of any account left.

There are a great many ways for spirits to communicate with mortals, but it is always through a medium of some kind, and though mortals are generally used as mediums, yet they are not always, as spirits sometimes use articles or pieces of furniture, through which to communicate with those in earth-life. Thus we read in the Scriptures that some consulted oracles, such as the Urim and Thummim, the Divining Rod and Divining Cup. Malcolm's Bible Dictionary says, "It seems probable that they (the Urim and Thummim) were the twelve precious stones of the high priest's breast-plate, on which were engraven the names of the tribes of Israel, and that the letters, by standing out, or by an extraordinary illumination, marked such words as contained the answer of God to him who consulted this oracle."

The Divining Rod, or Staff, is mentioned in Hosea 4:12. The cup which was placed in Benjamin's sack (Gen. 44:1 to 5) was a divining cup used by the king. Joseph also used divination. (See 15th verse of this chapter). These were used to receive communications from the spirit-world, the same as Planchette, Od-Graph, Psyche, and various other instruments are used by those who are mediums—mediumistic enough to get communications through them to day.

Nearly every one has some mediumistic qualities, which by time and perseverance could be developed. The following are the phases of mediumship to be found among mediums today, which we will take up in their order, and confirm them by Scripture proof : Clairvoyance, or clear seeing ; Seership, or foretelling of future events ; Clairaudience, or clear hearing ; Giving of tests, or test mediumship , Inspirational speaking,or speaking under spirit control; Divining; Healing by laying on of hands; by Fabrics, Languages Spoken, Trance, Slate Writing, Mind Reading, Spirit Writing, Levitation, or movement of bodies without physical contact, Transfiguration, Materialization.

CLAIRVOYANCE.

The Apostle Paul, in enumerating the gifts of the spirit, I Cor. 12:10, says : "To some is given the discerning of spirits." What will those who would have us believe that spirits and angels are two distinct orders of beings do with this passage? If spirits are only those who have passed from the mortal life, then this passage speaks of clairvoyance. In Numbers, 22d chapter, we have a case of clairvoyance. Several times in Verses 23 to 30 we read how Balaam's ass saw an angel in the way. In Verse 30 the ass is represented as speaking. About this time Balaam himself became clairvoyant. "And the Lord opened the eyes of Balaam, and he saw the angel of the Lord standing in the way, and his sword in his hand."—Verse 31. Here Balaam's inner vision is opened. In II Kings, 6th chapter, is another case of clairvoyance.

"The king of Syria wared against Israel, and took counsel with his servants, saying, in such and such a place shall be my camp" (Verse 8). In 9 and 10 Elisha warns the king of Israel, saying, "Beware that thou pass not such and such a place, for thither the Syrians are come down," thereby saving the life of the king of Israel. In Verse 11 the king of Syria calls his servants "and said unto them, will ye not tell me which of us is for the king of Israel." Verse 12 says : "And one of his servants said, none my Lord, O king; but Elisha, the prophet that is in Israel, tells the king of Israel the words that thou spakest in thy bed chamber." In Verses 13 and 14, the king of Syria sends horses and chariots, and a great host to Dothan to take Elisha prisoner. In the morning Elisha's servant finds the city compassed about with a great army, and asks, "Alas, my master! what shall we do?" (Verse 15). In 16 and 17 Elisha answers, "Fear not, for they that are with us are more than they that be with them," and the Lord opened the eyes of his servant in answer to Elisha's prayer, and he *saw*, and beheld the mountain was full of horses and chariots of fire round about Elisha."

Here we find the inner, spiritual vision opened. In 32 and 33, Elisha has a sitting at his house, and there fortells to those sitting with him that the messenger of the king is on his way to take his head, "and while he yet talked with them, the messenger came." Stephen, the first Christian martyr, when dying had his inner vision opened, and saw into heaven.—Acts 7:55:56. Job saw a spirit.—Job 4:14:15. He says : "Fear came upon me, which made all my bones to shake, then a spirit passed before my face; the hair of my flesh stood up." If angels and spirits are two distinct orders of creation, as some would have us believe, then this is a clear case of spirit return, and clairvoyance.

SEERSHIP, OR FORETELLING OF FUTURE EVENTS.

Seership, or foretelling of future events, is often mentioned in the Bible. The following are a few instances only: I Sam. 9:1 to 3, we learn that the asses of Kish, Saul's father, were lost. In the third verse, Kish sends his son Saul with one of his servants to seek the asses. After seeking in vain for the asses, Saul, with the servant, is about to return, when Saul bethinks himself that at Zuph there is a man of God that can foresee and foretell things, and adds, "All that he saith cometh surely to pass." (4th to 6th verses). From the 8th to 19th verses, we learn that they consult the seer, paying him for his services; the one-fourth of a shekel of silver. In the 20th verse Samuel, the seer, reads the mind of Saul, and says, "As for thine asses that were lost three days ago, set not thy mind on them for they are found." This is a clear case of fortune telling for money. In the 9th of this chapter we learn that it was customary to enquire of God through these seers. "Beforetime in Israel, when a man went to enquire of God, thus he spake, Come and let us go to the seer, for he that is now called a prophet, was beforetime called a seer." Instances of consulting these seers is found in I Chron. 21:9-11. It was customary for kings to have their seers, through whom they got communications from God. (Chron. 21:9 & 25:5) There are numerous gods mentioned in the Bible, but Jehovah was Israel's God. God is a spirit. (John 4:24). In Psalms 86:8 David compares the spirits, or gods, as follows : "Among the Gods there are none like unto thee, O Lord." In this the inspired writer acknowledges those other spirits to be gods, but his choice is Jehovah. Judges 11:24, the writer says : "Will not thou possess that which Chemosh *thy* God giveth thee to possess? So whomsoever the Lord *our* God shall drive out before us, them will we possess." See also Jer. 48:7; I Kings 11:33; II Kings 1:16. That there were other gods is also evident from the fact that Jehovah himself said : "Thou shalt have none other gods before me." (Deut. 5:7). "Every religion has its trinity of gods. The Hindu has its Brahma, Vishnu, and Siva, with a vast retinue of lesser divinities. Brahma was the creator, and Siva the evil one. In the theology of the Persians and their descendents, it was Ormuzd, Serosh, and Ahriman, with a host of subservient spirits. Ormuzd was the founder of the universe—the great, good, and all wise power. Serosh was the Messianic archangel, who directed lost souls to heaven, while Ahriman was the agent of destruction and wickedness."

"The Egyptians worshipped Osiris and Isis, and their trinity embraced Horus the avenger, conqueror of Typhon, restorer of life and the seasons, and the mediator between the upper and lower worlds. Among the Hebrews, Jehovah held the highest place in the pantheon of the deities, and the Romans worshipped Jupiter as the Heavenly Father, or the father of both gods and men.

"Thus we find very similar ideas and conceptions concerning the Divine Being, the Great Author of all things, and the lesser angels, divinities, and spirits existing among the various nations of antiquity." In Acts 14:8-13, we have an account of Paul's healing a man who was a cripple from his mother's womb. The 11th and 12th verses say : "And when the people saw what Paul had done, they lifted up their voices, saying in the speech of Lycaonia, The gods are come down to us in the likeness of men." "And they called Barnabas Jupiter, and Paul Mercurius, because he was the chief speaker." Verse 13 adds : "Then the priest of Jupiter, which was before their city, brought oxen and garlands unto the gates, and would have done sacrifice with the people." All beings who appeared to be supernatural in Bible times were taken for gods.

CLAIRAUDIENCE, OR CLEAR HEARING.

In I Sam. 3:4 to 10, we are told how the child Samuel heard spirit voices calling him three different times in succession. In the 9th chapter, 15th verse, we have another instance. "Now the Lord told Samuel in his ear a day before Saul came, saying, Tomorrow about this time, I will send thee a man out of the land of Benjamin, and thou shalt anoint him to be captain over my people Israel." Another instance still is that of Saul of Tarsus, mentioned in Acts 26:14: "And when we were all fallen to the earth, I heard a voice speaking unto me, and saying in the Hebrew tongue, Saul, Saul, why persecutest thou me?" And in Acts 11:7, "And I heard a voice saying unto me, Arise, Peter; slay and eat."

GIVING OF TESTS.

In I Sam. 10:1 to 8, we have a most remarkable test given through a test medium. After Samuel anoints Saul as Israel's king (read whole chapter), we find Samuel saying to Saul : "When thou art departed from me today, thou shalt find two men by Rachel's Sepulchre in the border of Benjamin at Zelzah, and they will say unto thee, The asses which thou wentest to seek are found, and lo, thy father hath left the care of the asses, and sorroweth for you, saying, What shall I do for my son? Then shalt thou go forward from thence, and thou shalt come to the plain of Tabor, and there shall meet thee three men going up to God at Beth-el, one carrying three kids, and another carrying three loves of bread, and another carrying a bottle of wine : And they will salute thee, and give thee two loaves of bread; which thou shalt receive of their hands. After that thou shalt come to the hill of God, where is the garrison of the Philistines : and it shall come to pass, when thou art come thither to the city, that thou shalt meet a company of Prophets coming down from the high place with a Psaltery, and a Tabret, and a Pipe, and a Harp before them, and they shall prophesy : And the spirit of the Lord shall come upon thee, and thou shalt prophesy with them and shalt be turned into another man : And let it be, when these signs are come unto thee, that thou do as occasion serve thee, for God is with thee : And thou shalt go down before me to Gilgal; and, behold, I will come down unto thee to offer burnt offerings, and to sacrifice sacrifices of peace offerings : Seven days shalt thou tarry, till I come to thee, and show thee what thou shalt do." Verse 9 says : "And it was so, that when he had turned his back to go from Samuel, God gave him another heart : And all these signs came to pass that day." In I Kings 14:1 to 6 is another remarkable test, given to the wife of Jeroboam the king. The son of Jeroboam was sick, and the wife of Jeroboam the king disguises herself at her husband's request, and taking ten loaves of bread, some cracknels, and a bottle of honey, with which to pay an old blind prophet—seer, or medium. It may not have been very popular to consult mediums in those days, so she disguised herself, as many do today when consulting mediums. In Verse 6 we are told that, "When Ahijah heard the sound of her feet, as she came in at the door, that he said, Come in thou wife of Jeroboam; why feignest thou thyself to be another? for I am sent to thee with heavy tidings." After giving her a message, giving tests concerning the overthrow of her husband's kingdom, he finally concludes his message, in Verse 12, as follows : "Arise thou therefore, get thee to thine own house; and when thy feet enter into the city thy child shall die." In Verse 17 the historian tells us that when she came to threshold of the door the child died, and if we read the history further we will find that every point in these predictions met a literal fulfillment.

INSPIRATIONAL SPEAKING.

Inspirational speaking, or speaking under spirit control, is quite frequently mentioned in the Scriptures. Many of our mediums never know a single word that they utter when delivering an inspirational address, while others are in a conscious state, but have no control of their vocal organs while speaking. We believe the same to be true of those who prophesied, or spoke under spirit control in Bible times. We may infer from Num. 22:38 that Balaam the prophet had no power to utter other than the words the Lord spake through him. In I Sam., 10th chapter, Samuel anoints Saul and foretells that Saul is to become a prophet—seer, and in the 6th verse says : 'And the spirit of the Lord shall come upon thee, and thou shalt prophesy with them, (the company of prophets mentioned in 5th verse) and thou shalt be turned into another man." Saul was not himself while under spirit control. Should any medium today be controlled to do what Saul did, (I Sam. 19:24) the Christian Church would lift up its hands in "holy horror" and denounce mediumship as the work of an orthodox devil, yet we are told (Verse 23) that it was that spirit spoken of so often in the Bible as God. Any message coming from a spirit source through a prophet—seer— was supposed to come from a god.

Thus we read of the prophets of the Lord, the prophets of Baal, and other prophets. We are sometimes asked why it is that our mediums commit errors at times in their prophesies. "Spirits themselves, through much more acute in their perceptions of the future than mortals, are but human. True and reliable prophesies can come from only very high spirits. Isaiah or Jeremiah could make false prophesies and still hold the seat of honor as God's prophets. Isa. 17:1 declares that Damascus shall be "a ruinous heap" and Jeremiah predicts its destruction by fire, and yet it stands up to this very time as a superb commercial city, which, according to Burckhardt, has a population of a quarter of a million." In Ezek. 2:2 we have a case of a spirit entering into Ezekiel, and using his vocal organs, spoke unto the prophet. "And he said unto me, Son of man, stand upon thy feet, and I will speak unto thee. And the spirit entered into me when he spake unto me, and set me upon my feet, that I heard him that spake unto me." Acts 19:13 to 16, we read of a case where an *evil* spirit spoke through the organism of a mortal. "Then certain of the vagabond Jews, exorcists, took it upon them to call over them which had evil spirits, the name of the Lord Jesus, saying, We adjure you by Jesus whom Paul preacheth, And there were seven sons of one Sceva, a Jew, and chief of the priests which did so. And the evil spirit answered and said, Jesus I know, and Paul I know, but who are ye?" In Acts 2:4 we read, "And they were all filled with the Holy Ghost, and began to speak with other tongues (no rare thing among mediums today) as the spirit gave them utterance."

In comforting the disciples against persecutions, Jesus, in Matt. 10:19:20 says, "But when they deliver you up, take no thought how, or what ye shall speak : For it is not 'ye that speak, but the spirit of your Father that speaketh in you." In Mark 16:17, in enumerating the signs that should follow them that believed in his name, Jesus told his disciples that "they shall speak with new tongues." Acts 19:6 says, "And when Paul had laid his hands on them, the Holy Ghost came on them, and they spake with tongues, and prophesied." Again, in Luke 21:14 and 15, after telling his disciples how they should be brought before kings and rulers for his sake, Jesus tells them, "Settle it therefore in your hearts, not to meditate before what ye shall answer : For I will give you a mouth and wisdom, which all your adversaries shall not be able to gainsay nor resist."

DIVINING.

In Gen. 44:1 to 5, we learn that the silver cup belonging to Joseph, which he caused to be placed in Benjamin's sack, was used by king Pharaoh as a divining cup, and in the 15th verse we learn that Joseph himself—one of God's best boys—practiced divination. In Numbers 22:7 we are told that in coming to Balaam—one of God's prophets—"The elders of Moab, and the elders of Midian took with them the rewards of divination." Balaam himself, though a prophet of God, sought enchantment. (Numbers 24:1.)

HEALING BY LAYING ON OF HANDS.

Acts 28:8:9 reads : "And it came to pass that the father of

Publius lay sick of a fever, and of a bloody flux, to whom Paul entered in, and prayed, and laid his hands on him, and healed him. So when this was done, others also which had diseases in the island, came, and were healed." After Christ had arisen from the dead, he appeared unto the eleven as they sat at meat: "And he said unto them, Go ye into all the world, and preach my gospel unto every creature. And these signs shall follow them that believe, In my name shall they cast out devils (evil spirits). They shall speak with new tongues. They shall take up serpents, and if they drink any deadly thing, it shall not hurt them, they shall lay hands on the sick, and they shall recover. (Mark 16:15:17:18).

Should one have those gifts today in the Church, that one would be turned over to the spiritualists as one who is linked in with the devil. There are scores of such healers in the ranks of spiritualism today, but the Church has lost the power to heal, because they have lost the Christ spirit. Healing is one of the gifts mentioned by Paul, in his letter to the Corinthians (1 Cor. 12:9). In chapter 14:1 Paul exhorts to "Follow after charity, and desire spiritual gifts."

HEALING BY FABRICS.

Acts 19:11:12, "And God wrought special miracles by the hands of Paul, so that from his body was brought unto the sick handkerchiefs, or aprons, and the diseases departed from them, and the evil spirits went out of them. There are thousands today in the world that can testify that they have been cured by wearing pieces of flannel which had been magnetized by healing meduims, and sent sometimes great distances through the mails. I know that many sceptics will laugh at the idea of such a thing, but psychometry has demonstrated that our magnetism is conveyed to every thing with which we come in contact.

LANGUAGES SPOKEN.

It is a frequent thing for mediums under spirit control to speak in—to them—unknown tongues. In Acts 2:5:8, we learn that at Pentacoste "There were dwelling at Jerusalem Jews, devout men, out of every nation under heaven : Now when this was noised abroad, the multitude came together, and were confounded, because that every man heard them speak in his own language : And they were all amazed and marveled, saying one to another, Behold, are not all those which speak Galilaeans ? And how hear we every man in our own tongue, wherein we were born ?

TRANCE.

The trance is one of the most common phases of mediumship. The subjebct sometimes being fully entranced will leave the body and visit distant localities. John O. Wattles, of Kansas, well known in the west as one of the most eloquent and earnest laborers in the antislavery cause, at a time when to be such was to be ostracised, accidentally discovered that his spirit could at will leave the body and return, and he frequently looks down as a spectator upon his body lying in a death-like trance, and then roams at pleasure over the earth, and returns again. Prof. William Denton, in a little book—"Is Spiritualism True" (Page 18) says: "Mrs. Cridge, Mrs. Denton, and my son Sherman, travel spiritually with great ease, and describe with great accuracy distant localities never visited by them." Dr. A. J. Davis, of Boston, Mass., also enters what he terms the "Superior State," in which he leaves the body and visits the spirit world at will.

There are hundreds of trance mediums today in the world. Acts 22:17, we learn that Paul fell into a trance while praying in the temple. While in the trance state the medium often describes the glories of the celestial country, and gives the names and description of loved ones who have lain off the mortal, and passed to that beautiful country. In II Cor. 12:2:4, Paul, in writing to the brethren says, "I knew a man in Christ above fourteen years ago (whether in the body I cannot tell, or whether out of the body I cannot tell; God knoweth); such an one caught up to the third heavens. And I knew such a man (whether in the body or out of the body, I cannot tell, God knoweth); How that he was caught up into Paradise, and heard unspeakable words, which it is not lawful for a man to utter."

Paul in making his "defense" before the "chief captain," and rehearsing his history, says, "And it came to pass that when I was come again to Jerusalem; even while I prayed in the temple, I was in a trance." (Acts 22:17). Again, Acts 10:9, "Peter went up on the house to pray about the sixth hour, and became very hungry, and would have eaten, but while they made ready, he fell into a trance, and saw heaven opened." Paul was doubtlessly entranced when he was "caught up into the third heaven," for he says he could not tell whether he was in or out of the body at that time.

SLATE WRITING.

This is one of the finest phases of mediumship that can be developed, as it is one of the most convincing, when coming through a genuine medium. In Exodus 31:18 we read : "And he (the Lord) gave unto Moses, when he had made an end of communing with him upon Mount Sinai, two tables of testimony, tables of stone, written with the finger of God." (See also Exodus 24:12, Deut. 4:13).

A slate is a table of stone and whether Moses ever received a communication from a spirit, I do not know. (God is a spirit; John 4:24). The orthodox Christian believes he did, though the account of it was recorded so long after the death of Moses that the historian says : "No man knoweth of his sepulchre unto this day." (Deut. 34:6).

To me it is the most likely thing in the world. On the 23d of June, 1891, I met my mother in materialized form at Mrs. Cadwell's, in N. Y. City, and talked with her, she greeting me with all the tenderness of a mother's love. In the evening of the same day, I, in company with John Fortune and another friend from Shamokin, visited Mrs. Mott Knight to get a sitting with her for "Slate Writing." Neither of us ever met her before and as she knew nothing of the questions we were to ask, or of our spirit friends, she therefore had no way of making any preparation or of preparing the messages beforehand, as some people would have us believe they do. On taking our seats at the table, the medium gave us each three slips of paper upon which we were to write our questions, addressing them to our friends in spirit-life, saying, as she did so, that we should turn the written side of our slips down upon the table. The medium then left the room until our questions had been prepared. During the medium's absence we turned the little table upside down, and a thorough examination of the same satisfied us that so far as the table was concerned there certainly was no chance for deception or fraud.

The medium soon entered the room to see if we were ready and taking her seat at the table told us to pick our slates from the little stand a few feet away from the table, upon which were placed a dozen or more slates. The medium then asked each in turn which of the slips we wanted answered first. Mr. Fortune's first question read : "If my father is present with me and can give me a message from spirit-life, please do so with your signature." To this question Mr. Fortune signed no names so that the medium had no way of knowing his or his father's, name. Mr. Fortune was then requested to place his slate upon his own hand and hold it under the table, with the upper surface of the slate against the under side of the table. The medium sitting on the opposite side of the table then placed her left hand on the table, while her right hand was placed under

Mr. F's hand, beneath the slate. Writing was immediately heard, followed by raps upon the slate. Upon examination the following message appeared upon the slate :

> MY DEAR BOY :
> This will come to your town some time.
> Your Father,
> JOHN FORTUNE.

Upon my first slip I asked mother for a few words from spirit life and upon my slate obtained the following :

> MY DEAR SON :
> I am not as strong as I was to day.   Amanda can write you.
> MOTHER.

I want to say that I met both Amanda (my brother Stephen's first wife) and mother that day at Mrs. Cadwell's, a few hours before receiving the messages on the slate.   The medium then told me to take two slates instead of one, which I did, receiving two messages, one being from my father and the other from Amanda.   The message from father was as follows :

> MY DEAR LEWIS :
> I am so glad, for we are all helping to convince the world of this grand truth.   William will some time believe in this.
> FATHER.

The William referred to is my brother, who had just begun to investigate, but who, at that time, was not fully convinced of the truth of spirit return.   These messages prove to my mind that those who loved us before the mortal form went down into the darkness of the tomb still live and live to love us.

Mr. Charles Watkins, of Cleveland, Ohio, now of Ayer, Mass., the wonderful medium for obtaining slate writing between closed slates, was severely tested by the Rev. Joseph Cook and a party of five sceptics in the library of Epes Sargent in Boston, Mass.   The committee certified "that two slates were clamped together with strong brass fixtures and held at arm's length by Mr. Cook, when a message was found on the inner surfaces." If these messages were not from a spirit source whence are they.   Our orthodox friends will no doubt say that Moses obtained his from God and that ours are from the devil.

MIND READING.

The people of Shamokin have had such convincing proof of

the genuineness of this phase of mediumship through Prof. H. Calif that it seems almost useless to say anything in connection with this phase, but we will say that there are hundreds of mind readers in the ranks of spiritualism today. Cases of mind reading I have already given under the head of Seership; we will recall a few of them.

In I Sam., 9th chapter, we have the account of Saul's visit to Samuel the seer, to consult him in regard to his father's asses which are lost. Saul met Samuel, and not knowing who he was, said unto him (18th verse) : "Tell me, I pray thee, where the seer's house is." In Verses 19:20 we read, "And Samuel answered Saul, and said, I am the seer : go up before me unto the high place, for ye shall eat with me today, and tomorrow I will let thee go, and will tell thee all that is in thy heart: And as for thine asses that were lost three days ago, set not thy mind on them, for they are found." In II Kings, 6th chapter, the king of Syria wars against the king of Israel. In the 11th verse, the king of Syria calls his servants "and said unto them, Will ye not tell me which of us is for the king of Israel." Verse 12, one of his servants said, "Elisha, the prophet that is in Israel, tells the king of Israel the words that thou speakest in thy bed-chamber."

People who know nothing concerning these "spiritual gifts" naturally think that Elisha was one of the most wonderful men that ever lived. A medium living in Ohio saw the danger that was menacing the late Jas. A. Garfield and went to Washington to warn him. He had an interview with the martyred President and forecast the future for him and told him that unless he exercised extraordinary precaution and care he would surely be assassinated. The President received the messenger most tenderly, but did not deem the message of suffcent importance to act upon its suggestions, hence the assassination that followed and which possibly might have been prevented.

Marguerite St. Omer, test medium, attended a meeting June 7th, 1891, at Hanson, Mass., where Dr. H. B. Storer was lecturing. On their return home it was reported that a young man had been drowned on Friday and his body could not be found. They called at the house where the young man used to board. She said, "I see the young man. He was about 25 years old, was a good swimmer. You need not send to Boston for a diver for he is only 15 feet from the point of land, and when they pull him out they will hook him in the eye." This was reported to them and in a few minutes they pulled him out. The Boston Daily Globe had the following: "It is stated that a clairvoyant told the searches where to look."

SPIRIT WRITING.

Mediums for this phase are many. One of the most remarkable instances of spirit writing is to be found in II Chron. 21:12-15. Here Elijah the prophet writes a letter to Jehoram, king of Judah, eleven years after his—Elijah's—translation. The translators of the King James Version have tried to cover up this fact by stating in the margin that the letter was written before Elijah's death.

There are two Jehorams, one was the son of Ahab, who reigned in the latter part of Elijah's life on earth. The other was the son of Jehoshaphat, and did not enter upon his reign until seven years after Elijah's translation, and reigned eight years. We learn that this Jehoram was Jehoshaphat's son, from the statememt made in the letter: "Because thou hast not walked in the ways of Jehoshaphat thy father," &c. Again, the translators must have forgotten that Elijah was translated without tasting death. Another proof that this writing was given after Elijah's translation we get thus: II Chron. 20:31, we learn that Jehoshaphat reigned over Judah 25 years. II Kings, 2, we have the account of Elijah's translation. In Chapter 3, 1st verse, Jehoram, the son of Ahab, began to reign—which is eight years after Elijah's translation—over Israel. At this time (1st verse) Jehoshaphat had reigned but 18 years, having yet to reign seven years to fill up his 25 year's reign. At the end of his reign—seven years after Elijah's translation—according to II Chron. 21:1, Jehoram, son of Jehoshaphat, began to reign in his father's stead, and the 5th verse says that he reigned eight years in Jerusalem.

According to the 18th and 19th verses of this chapter the Lord smites him with a disease from which he dies at the end of two years. As a great part of his wicked reign was before receiving this writing—Verses 12 to 15—we may safely place the receiving of it about the fourth year—or middle—of his reign, which four years added to the seven year's reign of Jehoshaphat, his father, after the translation of Elijah, would just make the eleven years between Elijah's translation and the receiving of this writing by Jehoram. Further proof that this writing came from Elijah, after Jehoram began to reign, is the fact that his wicked reign is spoken of in the letter, or writing.

The Bible, therefore, clearly proves and sanctions—

    1st—The communications of those who have passed to spirit life.

    2nd—That spirit writing is proven beyond a doubt by Biblical history.

In Daniel, 5th chapter, we have another case of spirit writing. A materialized hand writes upon the walls of Belshazzar's palace the words "Mene, Mene, Tekel, Upharsin." Both these wicked kings are reproved for their wicked acts and warned of their approaching destruction. Other cases of spirit writing could be given from the Bible, but these two should be sufficient to establish the fact that spirits can and do communicate with mortals. Let those who wish to pursue the subject further examine I Chron., 28th chapter, where a spirit writing is given to David, giving the pattern of the temple and its furniture. It was written by God's sanction and direction. Therefore, God sanctions spirit writing.

LEVITATION, OR THE MOVEMENT OF HEAVY BODIES.

This cannot properly be classed among the phases of mediumship, but is liable to take place in the presence of any medium, or in any circle of investigators. At the home of an intimate friend of mine—Edwin Worman, of Boonton, N. J.—I saw a table lifted midway between the floor and ceiling of the room during a sitting. John Fortune threw himself bodily across the table, but it was raised with him on it. Three persons then caught hold of the table, and such a tussling match as they had I never witnessed before, nor since. Among those that witnessed this was Joseph Cardwell, of Shamokin, who, I think, was one of the three who tussled with the table, which toward the last turned upside down, with its legs pointing toward the ceiling.

Magnetism! says some "smart Aleck." I afterward saw the same table leave the centre of the room and by request go to some of the sitters, no one being within ten feet of the centre of the room, and saw it answer questions intelligently by rising on its two legs and descending again upon the floor, three times for yes, twice for no, once for doubtful or don't know. You may gather in one all the magnetism in the universe and all the electricity that all the dynamos in the world could generate and apply it to lifeless, inert matter and it could not beget reason nor cause one intelligent movement. But there is an intelligent force manifested in the movement of a table when the letters of the alphabet needed to spell out a communication from a loved one in spirit life are rapped out, and that intelligent force is spirit.

It is a frequent thing for mediums to be lifted and carried about the room without physical contact. At a meeting of the "Society for Psychic Research," Mrs. Flower, wife of B. O.

Flower, Editor of the "Arena," was lifted, with a rocking chair in which she was sitting, and placed on a table, in the presence of many witnesses. I would state that this society is composed mainly of Ministers of the Gospel, the object of the society being to investigate Psychic Phenomena. An account of the above was given in the "Philadelphia Press" shortly after it occurred.

Levitation is several times referred to in the Bible. The following are a few instances : "And it shall come to pass, that as soon as I am gone from thee, that the Spirit of the Lord shall carry thee whither I know not." (I Kings 18:12). "And it came to pass, as they still went on, and talked, that, behold, there appeared a chariot of fire, and parted them both asunder; and Elijah went up by a whirlwind into heaven."—(2 Kings 2: 11). "Then the spirit took me up, and I heard behind me a voice of a great rushing." (Ezek. 3:12). "So the spirit lifted me up, and took me away." (Ezek. 3:14). "The Spirit of the Lord caught away Philip, that the eunuch saw him no more; and he went on his way rejoicing; but Philip was found at Azotus: And passing through he preached in all the cities till he came to Caesarea." (Acts 8:39:40).

TRANSFIGURATION.

Many times has this phase of phenomena been produced where the medium has been transfigured and led out into the room in an unconscious state, and claiming at such time to be a friend who has passed to spirit life. Should some one at such time seize the form they would find it to be that of the medium, while the spirit is just as truly the one it claims to be, as it would be, if it came in a body materialized for the purpose.

The Rev. C. H. Fitzwilliam once told me that if he ever had the opportunity of attending a materializing seance that he would have blood, if there was any. If he failed to get that, then he would be satisfied that it was a genuine spirit manifestation. He also told others that he would want the privilege of firing a revolver at the head of a form and if it failed to kill he would then believe it was a spirit. As the spirit draws upon the very life-forces of the medium to materialize its form, any injury done the form *must* and *will react* upon the medium and produce ofttimes fatal results, except where the medium and the spirit are made aware of the tests to be applied, then the controls will prepare for it by severing, for the time being, the battery between them and the medium, the medium regaining his or her normal condition.

I have many times known this to occur where sceptical persons have been permitted to put a finger in the eye of the materialized form. This was done in my own home on two different occasions, at one seance there being twenty-three persons present, at another twenty-nine persons. One of the persons thus privileged, after admitting the fact to certain ones, afterward denied it to others. Spirits reading the mind of a sceptic very often use such means to convince them that they are really what they claim to be—materialized spirit forms.

In enumerating the signs that should follow those that believe in his name, Jesus says, in Mark 16:18, "They shall take up serpents, and if they drink any deadly thing it shall not hurt them." I wonder how many could submit to the above Scripture test to prove their genuineness as Christians. If a *genuine* Christian, there certainly could come no harm from such a testing. I would make no mention of this passage but for the unreasonable tests asked for as to the genuineness of spirit manifestations.

On the 17th of May, 1890, at 9:45 A. M., my mother left her mortal form. At 11:30 I took the train at Boonton, N. J., and went thirty-three miles to attend a materializing seance at Mrs. Cadwell's, in the city of Brooklyn, N. Y. The medium never saw me before that time, had no way of knowing that I was to visit her that day, nor of my mother's having passed to spirit life that morning. At that seance my mother materialized, and coming from the cabinet, threw both arms about my neck, kissed me, and exclaimed, "God bless you, my dear boy!" She then spoke of her children, saying, "Tell William, Emma, Augusta, and the rest not to mourn so for me for I am through my suffering and am perfectly happy where I am."

On the 24th of Dec., 1889, at Mrs. Gray's, 323 W. 34th Street, New York City, I saw—fully ten feet away from the cabinet— within five feet of my eyes, a form rise apparently out of the floor, assuming gradually the form of a lovely female, giving the name of "Star Eye." I spoke to her, felt her hand, heard her speak as one in the mortal form would do, then watched the same form dematerialize again, standing on the very spot where but a few moments before it—the spirit—had clothed itself in materiality. Finally all had vanished except a luminous spot about the size of a ladies' handkerchief. Gazing intently upon this I beheld, gradually developing, the head of a man, then the shoulders, arms, and finally the whole form of an old gentleman, giving his name as Dr. Baker. I heard him answer questions put to him in regard to things on the spirit side of life and saw him disappear again as mysteriously as he came. I examined the carpet on that floor and found it to be whole. I never think of those two forms coming up, apparently through the floor, without thinking of the words of the woman of En-dor in answer to Saul's question: "What sawest thou?" "I saw gods ascending out of the earth."

If prejudice is cast aside and perfect conditions are given, our loved ones are ever ready to give us satisfactory evidence of the *fact* that spirits do return to mortals. Some people will sneer if told that it requires perfect harmony for spirit manifestations and yet those very persons, before a revival of religion, will spend a week in prayer and exhortation, getting the members of their church of one mind and in perfect harmony with each other, and when those conditions *are met*, who ever heard of that church failing to receive a baptism of the spirit?

We have one case of transfiguration mentioned in the Scriptures, in Mark 9:2:3, which reads: "And after six days Jesus taketh with him Peter, and James, and John, and leadeth them up into an high mountain apart by themselves: And he was transfigured before them: And his raiment became shining, exceeding white as snow, so as no fuller on earth could white them." And there appeared unto them Elias with Moses: And they were talking with Jesus." This spiritual manifestion must indeed have been grand. "And Peter answered and said unto Jesus, Master, it is good for us to be here: and let us make three tabernacles; one for thee, and one for Moses, and one for Elias." We can enter most fully into the feeling of Peter at this time, for who is there that ever attended a seance where they have met and talked with their loved ones whom death for a short time has seemed to separate from us, who has not felt as did Peter; but they soon vanish from our sight again. "And suddenly, when they looked round about, they saw no man any more, save Jesus only with themselves." (Verse 8). How often have we witnessed just such scenes, but we are glad even for these occasional visits, knowing that it will not be long, at the longest, till we, too, shall lay aside this robe of flesh which, as Paul says, is only the house we live in, and be permitted to join them once more in the summerland where partings shall be no more.

MATERIALIZATION.

This is the crowning phase of all mediumship. Many will not believe that a spirit can take on a material body so as to become tangible to our sense of touch, and talk with those who are still on the earth plane because they know nothing of the laws governing this phase ef spirit return. Mrs. Cora L. V. Richmond says : "If you would know the laws governing materialization you would guard them as carefully, preserve the conditions as sacredly, treat them with the same kind of deference and the same kind of reason that you do the carefully prepared plate, the electric battery, the various refined and subtle processes of chemical science that are oftentimes experimented with a thousand times before there is one successful result. The matter of which these forms are composed are taken—First, and mainly, from the medium, whom they usually entrance; Second, from the parties present at the seance, who may be mediumistic, and from whom they draw, and from the atmosphere which contains the particles of matter that are being constantly thrown off from the bodies of every one present at the seance," and by the chemical and electrical manipulation of these atoms of matter, spirits do, in a very short time build up a body which, by the ordinary process of nature, would require years to produce.

Materialization may be classed under two different heads, viz: Partial and full form materialization. A case of partial materialization is mentioned in Dan. 5:5: "In the same hour came forth fingers of a man's hand, and wrote over against the candlestick upon the plaster of the walls of the king's palace, and the king saw the hand that wrote." There are thousands of living witnesses in the world to-day to this kind of spirit writing.

The following we quote from the "Religion of Spiritualism," by Rev. Samuel Watson. Page 61, he says: "I mention one of many incidents which have occurred in my own house. A Methodist preacher, a member of the North Miss. Couference, and his wife, were spending a few days with us. They occupied a room in the south end of the third story. About noon, on a clear day, a little girl came to see us. At my request she went up to the preacher's room, into which she had never been. His shawl was spread over a small writing table. A slate was held by her under the cloth, with a small piece of pencil on it. A materialized hand wrote a number of messages, which the preacher said were from his father, long since passed to the spirit-land. A hand bouble the size of the girl's was extended from under the shawl, showing it in sunlight some distance up the wrist. The hand shook hands with the minister, his wife, and others who were present. It possessed a strength which was tested stronger than one or two of those whom it embraced."

In the 18th chapter of Genesis we have a case of spirits taking on a material form. In the first verse, one claiming to be the Lord appears to Abraham. "And he lifted up his eyes and looked, and lo, three men stood by him: and when he saw them he ran to meet them from the tent door, and bowed himself toward the ground: And said, My Lord if now I have found favor in thy sight, pass not away, I pray thee from thy servant." (Verse 2 and 3). From 4th to 8th verse, Abraham washes their feet and prepares them a meal and they partook of it. I was once told when quoting this passage that it did not state that they had their feet washed, but their reply, "So do as thou hast said," in the latter part of the 5th verse, in answer to the words, "Let a little water,I pray you, be fetched, and wash your feet," proves this. It is immaterial who did the washing act; my point is to prove that these beings had materialized bodies.

A spirit body cannot partake of coarse material food. In the 19th chapter of this book, there came two angels to Lot, at even, as he sat in the gate of Sodom. These he addresses as "my lords," in the second verse. In Verses 2 and 3, "They wash their feet, and Lot made a feast, and did bake unleavened bread and they did eat," thereby proving that these heavenly visitants also had for the time being material bodies. We might go on to show that other of these messengers had bodies as tangible to the material touch and sense as are our own bodies to our sense and touch. But we will now examine carefully an account of a "Materializing Seance," in Bible times. In I Samuel, 28th chapter, we have an account of Saul's visiting a woman, who the translators of the King James Version have seen fit to call a witch, but in the Hebrew Scriptures is only spoken of as the "woman of En-dor,"—they being about as honest as a majority of the orthodox divines of to-day. In the 3d verse, after Samuel was dead, Saul banished all those that had familiar spirits, out of the land. In the 5th verse we read: "And when Saul saw the host of the Philistines, he was afraid, and his heart greatly trembled." Verse 6 adds: "And when Saul enquired of the Lord, the Lord answered him not, neither by dreams, nor by Urim, nor by prophets—or seers. (See I Sam. 9:9).

We now find that this Saul has at last to fall back upon the very class of people whom he has been persecuting—the poor mediums. In Verse 8, he disguises himself—as a great many people do to-day when going to a medium—after learning from his servant that there is a woman at En-dor through whose mediumship the departed ones can come back to this world and commune with those yet in the earth-life. He takes the night time for it. This seance is composed of, as far as we can learn from the historian, three persons. In the 11th verse the medium sks Saul, "Whom shall I bring up into thee?" "And he aid, Bring me up Samuel." "And when the woman saw iamuel she cried with a loud voice: And the woman spake to iaul, saying, Why hast thou deceived me? for thou art Saul." n the 13th verse, in answer to Saul's question, "What sawest hou" the woman replied, "I saw gods ascending out of the arth," thereby showing what I have before said, that these naterialized forms were called gods. From the 15th to 21st erse there is quite a lengthy conversation between Samuel and iaul, in which Samuel tells Saul that all his trouble has come bout through Saul's failure to execute the fierce wrath of the ,ord upon Amalek.

Let us see what the command of this "Lord" was concerning imalek. I Sam 15:3, "Now go and smite Amalek, and utterly lestroy all that they have, and spare them not; but slay both nan and woman, infant and suckling, ox and sheep, camel and ss." One of this "God's" commands was, "Thou shalt not :ill," and yet we find the most horrible, wholesale butcheries ommitted at the express command of this God. In the 19th erse Samuel tells Saul that on the morrow he and his sons hould be with him. If we read the remaining chapters of this iook we will find that on the morrow Saul and his three sons vere killed in battle, in exact fulfillment of the words of iamuel.

In Genesis 32:24 to 32 we have an account of one of these ieavenly visitants wrestling with Jacob. This could not have ieen done unless the spirit had been clothed with a tangible, naterial body. In Verse 24 this being is called a man. In /erse 30, Jacob concludes that he has really had a wrestling natch with the Creator, and Ruler of this Universe. "And acob called the name of the place Peniel: for I have seen God ace to face, and my life is preserved,"again showing that these eings were taken for gods.

We now come to a New Testament seance. In the 9th of 1ark we find that "Jesus taketh with him Peter, and James, nd John, and leadeth them up into an high mountain apart by hemselves: and he was transfigured before them. * * * .nd there appeared unto them Elias and Moses, and they were alking with Jesus." Here we have two spirit beings who had nce lived in the mortal, coming back to the children of earth, nd yet we find those who will tell us of "that bourne whence o traveler returns."

In closing this phase of mediumship, I will give a few xtracts from Rev. Thomas Colley's—A.M., late of the Royal

Navy—account, which he with others witnessed, and published in London, England, but which I copy from "The Religion of Spiritualism," a book written by the Rev. Samuel Watson, a Methodist minister of Memphis, Tenn., and for sale by Day & Pitman, No. 9 Bosworth St., Boston, Mass. The Rev. Thomas Colley is a Baptist minister, as is also the medium on this occasion—the Rev. Dr. Monck—who, by the way, is one of the greatest living mediums. Following are a few extracts published by J. Burns, London :

"Dr. Monck was again medium. Four of us constituted the circle, all in perfect rapport with our instrument, having that confidence in him which is of knowledge, which yet for the sake of others and the better to observe what transpired, did not prevent us from taking every care in the application of tests that should answer for the genuineness of the manifestations and satisfy the most exacting."

"The sitting was wholly for materialization and the first form that appeared was that of a child, as it were, as we on this side of eternity would say, about six or seven years of age. This figure, in view of all, grew out of the medium's left side as he stood before us. It had all the actions and ways of human childhood; clapped its little hands, pursed its mouth to kisses, and spoke in pretty accents, Dr. Monck, under control, speaking to it and instructing it like an elder brother; then after a few minutes' further stay, sliding back into the medium, it gradually disappeared.

"The next form was none other than Dr. Monck's old earth friend, fellow student, brother minister and chief spirit-control, Samuel Wheeler. When he, in like manner issuing forth, first stepped from the medium into separate being, Dr. Monck was unconscious, under control of 'Lily' and her voice through him contrasted very markedly with the voice of the materialized form—it, to the very syllable, being the voice of 'Samuel,' as when speaking through the medium. But this did not satisfy our spirit-friend, for the marvel of the night's effort had yet to culminate. Conditions being so good, 'Samuel' thought he might dematerialize and awake Dr. Monck, and then to be able to dematerialize with the medium in his normal state, fully alive to all that transpired, and conscious of the astounding fact we were to witness, and successful beyond all conception of the mystery, was this most unique experiment; for after the first alarm of Dr. Monck had passed away, and after the pain and nervous snatchings he felt in the process of his friend's evolution from himself had subsided, medium and spirit-form conversed naturally together, and the astonishment and glee of the former were only equaled by our profound sense of inability adequately to grasp at first the vast significance of this amazing demonstration of occult power. Equally with the child-form did Samuel Wheeler show all the attributes of humanity, and in his case, reason and ripe manhood, as in her's, girlishness and simplicity. He was not unlike the medium in stature, form, and bearing; and one of our company having intimately known 'Samuel', in the earth-life (being frequently one of his congregation when our spirit-friend was, as our medium also was, a Baptist minister), unhesitatingly declared that this 'Samuel Wheeler' was that 'Samuel Wheeler,' and none other.

"So for some time the spirit, temporarily clothed with earthly elements, molecular agglutinations and atomic gatherings, that thronging in from spirit—attraction and life—magnetism, clinging round the soul—Deity's central fact—form the visible man, the spirit thus endued, compacted, and embodied, stayed and talked with us, walked about with his old friend Dr. Monck, and greeted his other friend joyfully, and did many other things to show how perfectly he was a man, and then at last, psychological laws (about which we are altogether in the dark) compelling, reluctantly retired, and drifting back into the medium, threw him into trance and resumed control.

"And now a new sensation was in store for us. A spirit-form, eight inches taller than Dr. Monck, grew from him by degrees, and building itself up into giant proportions with muscular limbs, developed like statuary of bronze, and of the color, there came into disconnected, independent, vigorous life, apart from the medium, an ancient Egyptian. From its general aspect, dress and manner, I addressed it as such at once without a moment's doubt or hesitation. For ancient Egypt has been a favorite study with me, and in modern Egyptians I have, when in the East, endeavored to trace the ancient masters of Israel and the sciences, and have dreamed amid the ruins of the temple of Isis, and sketched the blue tuniced and turbaned descendant of the Pharaoh's, and have pleasant recollections of an Egyptian Fellah, Zozab, who used to accompany me through the bazaars, and pioneer me through the intricacies of Suez; and if ever Bulwer's Arbaces the Egyptian, in the "Last Days of Pompeii," had existence other than in the mind of the author, it was here embodied in the materalized form I handled and closely scrutinized last night.

"The vitality and power of this spirit were remarkable; it walked with manly step and dignified carriage round and about the room, before and behind us, without fear or hesitation; appeared curious about, and leisurely inspected the furniture and ornaments of the room; took up a chair and placed it on the table; brought us books and other things, and then, taking the chair from the table, placed it close to mine and sat down at my side. Meanwhile I closely introspected it and felt its anatomy, the medium standing at my left side while 'Mahedi' (the Egyptian) was seated at my right. I now got the spirit to measure hands, placing its palm on mine. The hand (stone cold, while the medium's was burning hot,) was small, like all Eastern's and the wrist was also small, but the arm was massive, muscular, bronzed, and hairy. Its eyes were black and piercing, but not unkindly; its hair lank and jet, and mustache and beard long and drooping, its features full of life and expression, yet Sphynx-like. Its head-dress was very peculiar, a sort of metal skull-cap with an emblem in front, overhanging the brow, which trembled and quivered and glistened. I was suffered to feel it, but as I did so it seemed to melt away like a snow-flake under my touch, to grow solid again the moment after.

"Altogether our mysterious visitant was a weird and everlasting puzzle. But for the sake of an inner circle studying with me the correspondence and causative philosophy of these mysteries, I am instructed to say that 'The Mahedi' is the 'Coming Phase,' and what I have thus been the first to witness has yet to develop to something out of all proportion to anything at present experienced or dreamt of.

"But other matters of moment transpired too recondite to be lucidly recorded, and at last our new acquisition from the 'Grand Man,' through mortal man retired, and bowed a silent adieu, and as I had done with other spirit-forms in their exeunt and exit, I, at the distance of a few inches only, watched 'The Mahedi's absorption into the body of the medium, and his gradual disappearance, till he was merged viewless into the boundless hereafter through this mortal gate of access to the mysteries of the other life.

"But Dr. Kennedy was now invited to draw equally near and realize more closely with me the marvel of the separate identity of the spirit-form from the medium, and as we stood looking with all our soul upon the mighty fact of *spirit birth from mortal man*, Dr. Monck, still entranced, placed the lovely visitant from the inner world between us, and affording it each the support of an arm, we advanced with our sweet spirit-companion some steps further into the room. Meanwhile, holding the hand of the spirit-arm that rested on mine, I felt the wrist, palm, fingernails; it was in every respect a living hand, answering to my touch, yielding to pressure, having natural weight and substance, and all things pertaining to humanity, but it was damp and stone cold and the thought passed through my mind, how, like steam, first invisible, congealed, is then seen as cloudy vapor, which, precipitated, may finally take solid form in ice, this figure at my side had, by a somewhat analogous process, been rendered visible and tangible from the vital force, viewless and imponderable, of the medium, being under the chemistry, not yet understood of the higher life, congealed into the nebulous condition instanced of the form's first appearance, further to solidify into the lovely· creature we supported and wistfully beheld. But, not to theorize, I now come to the climax of the night's most wonderful phenomena.

"When the form at last retired I was, as an extreme favor which might cause the medium great prostration, permitted to accompany it and draw near with it slowly and cautiously, until I came again close up to Dr. Monck, as he, still entranced, stood forth full in view of all, waiting to receive back into himself the marvelous aeon, phantasm or emanation that we *must* call angel or spirit. As it neared him the gossamer filament again came into view, its attenuated and vanishing point being, as before, toward the heart. By means of this subtle cord I noticed how this psychic figure seemed to be sucked back into the body of the medium. For like a water-spout at sea—funnel shaped—or sand column, such as I have seen in Egypt, horizontal instead of vertical, the superior vital power of Dr. Monck seemed to absorb and draw in the spirit form, but so gradually that I was enabled closely to watch the process; for, leaning against and holding the medium, with my left arm at his back, and my left ear and cheek to his breast, his heart beating in a most violent and alarming way, I saw him receive back the lovely birth of the invisible spheres into his very person and, as I gazed for the last time on the sweet face of the disintegrating spirit, within three or four inches of the features, I marked its fair aspect, eyes, hair, and delicate complexion, and kissed the dainty hand as, in process of absorption, it dissolved and saw the angel face disappear and fade, as it was drawn, positively, into the bosom of the medium. Gazing thus closely with awe and breathless interest, did I, therefore, watch the departure of our angel-friend, and the living gate and avenue of the medium's very self did I, with feelings indescribable, mark the steps of her progress to regain, through the living organism of Dr. Monck, her home in the viewless spheres."

Hon. A. H. Dailey, Ex-Judge of Surrogates, and the senior partner of one of the best known and most high-class firms in the legal profession in the city of Brooklyn, New York—Dailey,

Bell and Crane—in an interview with Walter Howell, published in "The Light of Truth," Cincinnati, Ohio, July 7, 1894, in speaking of Dr. Monck says: "I met Dr. Francis W. Monck first at the residence of Mr. Fred Haslam, in Brooklyn, about 1881, at a reception given to Dr. Monck by Mr. Haslam, and I became quite intimately acquainted with him. He was very poor, and a purse was made up and presented to him. He was seeking employment as a magnetic healer. I have witnessed some remarkable phenomena through his mediumship. His fame had, as a materializing medium in England, become known here. He gave a few seances in Brooklyn, but none for materialization. The phenomena usually consisted of raps, moving of heavy articles of furniture, and upon a few occasions of the passing of matter through matter. I will explain the remarkable experience we had with him when this was done. There were probably a dozen people present, seated at a large extension table with Dr. Monck in the circle. By very heavy raps in answer to the alphabet it was announced that matter would be passed through matter, under strictly test conditions. Among the most sceptical was the late Mr. S. B. Nichols, who did not believe it could occur, and I certainly could not conceive how it could be done, and I never could. All explananations have not explained to my comprehension. To be sure there was no deception, Dr. Monck was firmly held by both wrists by four persons, two holding each wrist or hand. Mr. Nichols and myself each held a wrist and we did it so firmly that the doctor complained of being hurt. All the rest in the circle were directed to sing and one to turn down the light. In an instant Dr. Monck uttered a groan, we heard a rustling sound, and the lights were at once turned up. We were still holding Dr. Monck firmly, but his coat, vest, and cuffs were gone from his person. His vest was over the head and face of Mr. Nichols, his coat was on the floor. His cuffs, still unbuttoned, were in different places in the room. We did not release our hold until every one present was satisfied that we had held him securely, and when we did do so, the firmness of our grip left deep impressions upon the doctor's wrists and hands; one of his fingers was bleeding from the cut of a ring pressed into the flesh.

Doctor Monck certainly had these articles on his person when we took hold of him. They were not torn or separated into parts when we again examined them as they were replaced upon his person. If anything seemingly set the laws of nature at defiance this did. I do not believe any person can be made to understand how those garments were removed; I have no doubt but we shall some time understand it, but not in this world.

The most satisfactory observation of the process of Materialization I have ever witnessed was with Dr. Monck. It was during a call at the house of Dr. Blake in Brooklyn. There were five persons present. My wife, Dr. Monck and I were passing Dr. Blake's residence one evening and made a social call. As an amusement we sat for a few moments at a round table to see what manifestations would be given. A gas jet was dimly burning directly over the table. An exclamation from Dr. Monck called attention to the formation of a dense vapory mass close to his side. It was in incessant agitation. The hands of each sitter were on the table in plain view. We looked at it intently, when it disappeared with the quickness of lightning. While we were dicussing the strange phenomena it re-appeared, and commenced forming the shoulders, arms, and vapory body of a human being, and again as quickly disappeared. This was repeated a number of times in the plain view of all. The effect upon Dr. Monck was quite serious, and produced a hemorrhage of the lungs, the same as had followed his materializing seances in England. The serious result prevented, in so far as I have known, the efforts of Dr. Monck to give materializing seances in this country."

Many persons do not believe that spirits are able to pass matter through matter as described above, but not less remarkable was the seance given in the G. A. R. Opera House in Shamokin, on the evening of Friday, Oct. 27th, 1894, by the two noted spiritual mediums, Ira T. Davenport and Mr. Fay. A. G. Marr, one of Shamokin's most prominent lawyers, and W. S. Guiterman, Editor of the "Daily Dispatch"—and who, by the way, with the assistance of "Detective" Henry Welker and a few of Shamokin's lesser lights, undertook about a year ago, the difficult task of killing Spiritualism in Shamokin— were appointed a stage committee, whose duty it was to make a thorough examination of the cabinet used by the mediums, to see that the seance was given under strict test conditions and to detect fraud, if any could be found. The committee, by request of Mr. Fay, examined the cabinet thoroughly, which, by the way, was a plain wooden structure about 5x9 feet, standing on long iron castors, leaving a space of from 12 to 15 inches under the cabinet, so that all persons sitting in the parquet could look under the cabinet throughout the entire cabinet seance—and reported that after thorough examination they found it to be a plain wooden structure very securely framed together and declared that they could discover no chance of fraud, so far as they could see. The mediums then took their seats, one in each end of the cabinet, facing each other. By request, the mediums were tied by the committee, who afterward reported to the audience that they had tied them hand and foot, as thoroughly as it was possible to do, with their hands tied behind their backs in such a manner that it was impossible for them to slip their hands from the ropes. Musical instruments, consisting of two guitars, several tambourines, bells, and some other instrument, where placed between the two mediums. The doors in front of the cabinet were then closed; but as the middle door of the three was being closed the manager requested Mr. Guiterman to take a final look to see if the men were still in their positions. As he did so he received a slap on the face from a hand inside the cabinet and was also hit on the head with a tambourine, leaving the tambourine strung about his neck, some one remarking, "A cuff and a collar the first go off."

Immediately after the doors were closed the instruments began to be rattled and banged about in the cabinet, the racket being kept up for several minutes, during which time hands of different sizes were shown from a small window in the middle door of the cabinet; on one occasion the arm of a female, bared to above the elbow, was thrust out of the window. No sooner had the sound of the instruments ceased than the doors of the cabinet were thrown open by some power from the inside and the committee found both mediums securely tied as before the doors had been closed. The attention of the committee, some time during the seance, was called to the fact that the locks were arranged in such a manner that it was impossible for the doors to be locked or unlocked except by physical contact, on the inside. After examining, Mr. Marr reported the fact to the audience. I make mention of this because it goes far towards showing that it could not have been done by the hands of the mediums, as it was utterly impossible for them to untie and tie in so short a time, or even for a confederate, could there have been one.

The mediums being still tied, the doors were again closed and locked from the inside. On taking a final look to see if the mediums were still bound, before closing the middle door, Mr. Marr this time, got a slap with the hand from the cabinet, a tambourine also being strung about his neck. In about as short a time as it would take to tell it the doors were thrown open and both mediums stepped from the cabinet untied, leaving the ropes lying in the cabinet. They again entered the cabinet, when they were as quickly tied again, this time by some invisible power in the cabinet—as the committee reported

—more securely than they could possibly tie them.

Mr. Guiterman was now ordered to take his seat in the cabinet between the mediums, facing the audience; a hand was placed upon each of the mediums and tied with ropes so as to detect any movement upon the part of either. The instruments were then placed upon Mr. Guiterman's lap, the doors were closed and immediately all the instruments in the cabinet were being played, hands being continually shown at the window. "You will observe," says Mr. Marr, "that the hands are smaller than those which we tied." After a time the music ceased, the doors were opened and Mr. Guiterman sat with a tambourine strung about his neck and the three men were found securely bound. At Mr. Fay's request, Mr. Guiterman gave his experience while in the cabinet, in substance as follows: "I took my seat in the cabinet, as you saw, with the instruments upon my lap, tied to both men. Could detect no movement on the part of either; a dozen hands were passed over my face, patting me on the back. Hands were thrust into all my pockets. Every request I made while in the cabinet was granted. Do not think it possible for the men to do it."

Mr. Marr was now requested to take his seat in the cabinet, the instruments were placed upon his lap, his hands were placed upon each of the mediums and tied. The doors were closed with the same result as when Mr. Guiterman was in the cabinet, except that Mr. G. got a slap on the head this time as the doors were being closed. Immediately after the noise of the instruments had ceased the doors were opened and Mr. Marr sat with a tambourine collar on, securely tied to both mediums. As the doors were locked in such a manner that they could only be unlocked from the inside by physical contact, and no movement could be detected by either committeeman on the part of the mediums, and both were found securely bound, it is evident that they were opened by some power other than the mediums. Mr. Marr reported his experience while in the cabinet, in substance as follows: "I took my seat in the cabinet; the instruments were placed on my lap. I held both men; could detect no movement on the part of either. The instruments were all playing. At my request they played above me in the cabinet. Hands were passed over my face and thrust in every pocket. I was completely deluged both with music and with instruments." This latter statement created much laughter. On being asked by Mr. Fay if he thought that they had anything to do with the manifestations Mr. Marr said, "I am unable to explain how they could have had anything to do with the manifestations. It is entirely beyond my comprehension. I am amazed." Says

Mr. Fay: "What do you say, Mr. Guiterman?" "The same as Mr. Marr," answered Mr. Guiterman.

The mediums being still tied, the doors were again closed for a few seconds, then they were opened and Mr. Fay stepped from the cabinet untied and to show the audience that they took no part in untying themselves, Mr. Fay, in the presence of the committee, placed a teaspoonful of flour in each of Mr. Davenport's hands—which also could be seen by the audience—the committee pronounced Mr. Davenport securely bound, the doors were closed, and in less time than any mortal could have done it, even in the light (the cabinet was dark inside) Mr. D. was untied, and stepping from the cabinet in the presence of the committee and in full view of the audience, opened his hands, which were found to contain the flour placed there by Mr. Fay a few moments before.

A DARK SEANCE.

Mr. Fay now stated that a dark seance would be given, but as it required perfectly negative conditions—stating that as it required darkness for the photographer, so it required the same negative conditions for this phenomena—yet the seance would be given under strict test conditions, as light would be admitted every few minutes, showing that there were no confederates and no deception.

Two chairs were now placed upon the stage. The mediums seated themselves and were again securely bound with ropes, by the committee, their hands being tied behind them in such a manner that it was impossible for them to get loose without the aid of a confederate. The lights were extinguished for a few seconds after which they were turned on again, when both mediums were found untied. Mr. Fay now stated that they would again be tied, but not by the committee this time. The lights were extinguished and in much less time than the committee could have done it, both mediums were again tied—by invisible agency this time—as Mr. Marr stated, more securely than they could bind them.

And now came the most mystifying phenomena of the evening—the passing of matter through matter. The feet of both mediums were placed upon white sheets of paper. With a lead pencil Mr. Marr drew the outline of Mr. Fay's shoes, likewise Mr. Guiterman of the shoes of Mr. Davenport, so that it would be impossible for them to move a foot in the dark without being detected. Mr. Marr was now requested to seal the knots which secured Mr. Fay to his chair. This was done with sealing wax, to the entire satisfaction of both committeemen.

The lights were extinguished. Mr. Fay told Mr. Marr to request that his coat be removed, which he did. Immediately light was called for and Mr. Fay sat before the audience in his shirt sleeves, his coat still flying through the air. The committee examined the knots and found them to be intact, with the seals unbroken, also examined the sheets of paper and found that the feet of neither had been moved. Mr. Guiterman was now requested to put Mr. Fay's coat upon himself, which he did, laying his own coat aside. The lights were extinguished and immediately called for again and Mr. Guiterman's coat was found upon the medium. The lights were again extinguished and in as quick time as before were turned on again, when Mr. Fay again sat in his shirt sleeves, while Mr. Guiterman's coat was seen flying through the air, landing on the foot lights.

At this juncture two more committeemen—H. G. Steel and Harry Leam—were called to the stage, the backs of the guitars were rubbed with a luminous oil, the instruments all being placed upon a table, the two last chosen committeemen stood, one at either end of the stage. Mr. Steel held the manager, Mr. Leam held Mr. Davenport, Messrs. Marr and Guiterman were seated at the table with Mr. Fay; Mr. Guiterman placed a foot upon both Mr. Fay's feet, his right hand was placed upon Mr. Fay's head, while Mr. Fay held tightly the wrist of the same, with both his hands, Mr. Marr also, from the other side, holding Mr. Fay, so that the least movement on his part might be detected. The lights were again extinguished, when again every instrument began moving about, playing, the illuminated guitars flying through the air at a terrific rate of speed, rising at the request of Mr. Marr to a distance of 8 or 10 feet in the air, now lower, then higher, passing back and forth, from one end of the stage to the other.

Light was called for, when the two guitars were thrown, landing with great force, one at the feet of Mr. Steel, the other at the feet of Mr. Leam. The committee were asked to report. They did so, stating that they could detect no movement on the part of Mr. Fay, Mr. Davenport, or the manager. At this juncture Mr. Fay thanked the audience for their kind attention and made the following statement. "There is no sleight of hand, no trickery, deception, nor confederates here tonight. We are not here to say what power has produced this, but leave each one to judge for themselves. Good night." The following appeared in the "Daily Dispatch" of the next day :

DAVENPORT AND FAY.

"Davenport and Fay mystified their audience at the Opera

House last evening by their wonderful and incomprehensible cabinet seances. Messrs. A. G. Marr and W. S. Guiterman were appointed a stage committee, and although they were tied in the cabinet with Davenport and Fay, they were unable to explain how the mysterious music and other manifestations were caused, when the performers were apparently bound."

Why do you say "apparently bound," Mr. Guiterman? If so, then you *apparently* bound them. They *were* bound. But whence those hands that slapped you and Mr. Marr on the face and strung the tambourines on your necks, that stroked your faces, slapped you on the back, were thrust in your pockets, that granted your requests while in the cabinet, that locked the doors from the inside, while the mediums were still bound, without a movement on their part, that tied the mediums even more secure in the dark and in a shorter time than you could even in the light, that showed themselves at the cabinet window, that untied the mediums in a much shorter time than you could, that removed the medium's coat and put your coat on the medium, with his hands and feet securely bound, without breaking the seals upon the knots, that played all those instruments while flying through the air at such a terrific rate of speed?

You say, "We are unable to explain." Will you please let one who, about a year ago, you called deluded, explain? The hands that did all this were none other than the materialized hands of a band of immortals, who once passed through this earth life as you and I are doing and who are trying to demonstrate to the world that "there is no such thing as death." You ask, "How is it done?" I answer, from the bodies of every person assembled there is constantly being thrown off through insensible perspiration, very finely attenuated particles of matter, and by a chemical and electrical manipulation of these atoms, together with other atoms that are constantly floating in space everywhere, the disembodied spirit is enabled to clothe itself with a real, tangible, material body. Mediums for materialization are those who possess a certain amount of what spirits themselves term psycho-dynamic power. Through this force—existing in the medium—spirits attract from the atmosphere these substances and particles. This process of materialization we can see going on all around us in nature. Every atom that shall go to compose next year's fruit now exists somewhere in the great ocean of matter that surrounds this world of ours.

Go with me in the spring when the buds begin to shoot forth

and follow this process of materialization. As the little buds burst a thousand tiny cups may be seen holding up their dainty heads, drinking in the sunshine of heaven. Within each little cup, hidden from mortal view, and placed there by an all-wise and provident God, is a little magnetic, spiritual germ, attracting to itself atom after atom of matter, from out the great ocean of matter surrounding it, until finally you behold the materialized, golden fruit. You partake of that fruit and your own immortal spirit within takes up those atoms of matter, and through a subtle process of spirit-chemistry of which, as yet, little is understood by mortals, is materialized the body that clothes your spirit; for remember, these bodies of ours are constantly dematerializing and would soon pass away were it not that this process of materialization is constantly going on from the food we eat. This process of materialization is going on all around us in nature. Indeed, you cannot point to a single material thing in all the vast universe of God but what has thus been materialized. "Through the existence and force of spirit operating throughout the universe, substance has been wrought upon. Atoms, elements and forces are brought together by the operation of the law of attraction, and assume shape, come into the form of objective life, but nevertheless they are vitalized by that inherent and potent force which we call spirit."

The whole world is beginning to realize that what we term spiritual phenomena are real. Even that great enemy of Spiritualism, T. De Witt Talmage, some time ago said in a sermon: "There is a class of phenomena that makes me think that the spiritual and the heavenly world may, after a while, make a demonstration in this world which will bring all moral and spiritual things to a climax. Now I am no spiritualist; but every intelligent man has noticed that there are strange and mysterious things which indicate to him that perhaps the spiritual world is not so far off as sometimes we coujecture, and that after a while from the spiritual and heavenly world there may be a demonstration upon our world for its betterment. We call it magnetism, or we call it mesmerism, or we call it electricity, because we want some term to cover up our ignorance. I do not know what it is. I never heard an audible voice from the other world. I am persuaded of this, however, that the veil between this world and the next is getting thinner and thinner, and that perhaps, after a while, at the call of God—not at the call of the Davenport Brothers, or Andrew Jackson Davis—some of the old spiritual warriors; some of the spirits of other days, mighty for God—a Joshua, or a David, or a Paul—may come down and help us in this battle against unrighteousness."

Should Joshua, David, Paul, and all the good men that ever lived from Adam to the present day come back to earth, the Rev. Talmage and his like would denounce their return as the works of the orthodox devil. Like the brethern of Dives of old, "neither will they be persuaded, though one rose from the dead."

Yes, dear reader, spirit-return is an established fact; materialization of spirit forms is a fact, and though there are frauds in the world who would deceive us, yet there are hundreds of good, genuine mediums. The Church may call spiritualism witchcraft, enchantment, divination, sorcery, dealing with familar spirits, or whatever they please. I have shown very clearly that every one of the phases of mediumship that are bestowed upon and practiced by our mediums to-day, were held and practiced by God's own children in Bible times. These different phases of mediumship are gifts from God. If a man or a woman has the gifts of Clairvoyance, Seership, Clairaudience, Giving of Tests, Inspirational Speaking, Divining, Healing, Speaking of Languages, Trance, Mind Reading, or any other of the many gifts of the spirit, they can no more help having those gifts than they can help breathing.

The apostle Paul, in his letter to the Corinthians, 14:1 says: "Follow after charity, and desire spiritual gifts." In the 12th chapter we read: "Now concening spiritual gifts, brethren, I would not have you ignorant. * * * Now there are diversities of gifts, but by the same Spirit. * * * But the manifestation of the spirit is given to every man to profit withal. For to one is given by the spirit, the word of wisdom; to another the word of knowledge by the same spirit; to another faith by the same spirit; to another the working of miracles; to another prophesy; to another discerning of spirits; to another divers kinds of tongues; to another the interpretation of tongues. But all these worketh that one and the selfsame spirit, dividing to every man severally as he will."

The Church has ever been ready to strangle any new truth, but her attitude toward Spiritualism is fast changing wherever it has been established and the time is coming when every church door will be opened for the utterance of its truths. The Church charges spiritualists with being indifferent to the truths of the Bible. This is a mistake. We accept all the spiritual facts of the Bible and stand by them, but we cannot accept the Bible as a whole in the sense that the Church does, knowing that it has its mistakes and its contradictions. It is not the sacred books of the world that are inspired, but the truths that they mirror forth. All the facts of Modern Spiritualism are established by the Bible. Ancient and Modern Spiritualism run on parallel lines; we cannot accept the old and ignore the new. The Church not only ignores the foundation of her faith—spirit manifestations and power—denying the possibility of the signs which Christ himself said should follow those that believe in His name, but she pronounces the wide-spread spirit manifestations to be of the devil. Is it not a significant fact that the Church does not possesss these gifts to-day, but that every one of them are possessed by those Spiritualists whom the Church to-day—if the laws of the country were such—would torture at the stake as witches, and all in the name of Christianity.

I have had persons say to me, Well, suppose Spiritualism is true, what good can it do? I would say that it has demonstrated what the Church for ages has been teaching, but has failed to prove—that man is immortal. Spiritualism has done more than all else combined to sweep back the tide of materialism which but a few years ago was sweeping over Europe and America. The Bible says "Add to your faith knowledge." The Church *believes* in man's immortality, but as soon as one of its members begins to seek for a knowledge of immortality they are told that it is sinful to "pry into the hidden things of God." There are millions of people to-day who know that spirit return is a fact, while thousands more believe it. Spiritualism robs death of its terrors, leads the thirsty to living waters, and lightens the burdens of weary pilgrims, and shows that death is but a beautiful transition or birth into a better life. It is the most joy-inspiring of religions, as it gives us back our loved and lost and proves the glorious life that awaits us. Spiritualism is built upon demonstrated facts.

Dr. J. P. Newman, the eloquent Methodist Episcopal Bishop, said some time ago, in a sermon delivered at a funeral, 561 Madison Ave., New York: "The two worlds met in Bible times. The communications were as real then between earth and heaven, as between New York and London to-day. From Adam till John of Patmos there was frequent intercourse between those who had gone and those who were left behind." Angels were companions of Daniel in the lion's den ; they conversed with Mary; they delivered Peter from prison; they visited Cornelius the Roman Centurion. Celestial visions were given to Isaiah and the prophets, to Paul and the apostles, to Stephen and the martyrs, while Samuel, and Moses and Elias were returned to earth. And why should we suppose that there is less interest in heaven for earth now than in the glorious past! We have the inspired record of the return of five persons to our earth, three of whom entered the spirit-world through the portals of the grave."

"And there was another who was born here, and went to that spirit-land and returned to us, and remained with us from June 44, A. D., till June 64, A. D., a period of twenty years; and six years after he made this declaration public. He said : "I was caught up into the third heaven." This is levitation as taught in I Kings 18:12; Ezak. 3:14, in Acts 8:39-40. He went not only to the place of departed spirits, but to Heaven, where he heard unspeakable words.

Do you say that if only one of our own race and time would go and return and witness to us it would be sufficient? Most lawyers are satisfied with one good witness. The law is that two good witnesses are sufficient to confirm a fact, but here are eight—Samuel, Moses, Elias, Christ, and four apostles. These eight persons are as good as eight hundred.

But do the communications between the two worlds continue to this day? Let us rise to the sublimity and purity of the great Bible truth, and on this day of sorrow console our hearts therewith. It was the opinion of Wesley that Swedenborg was visited by the spirits of his departed friends. Dr. Adam Clarke believed that the departed spirits returned to earth.

The sainted John Wesley remarked in one of his sermons (Vol. 2-470-1): "And how much will it add to the happiness of those spirits who are already discharged from the body, that they are permitted to minister to those whom they have left behind? An indisputable proof of this we have in the twenty-second chapter of the Revelation. When the apostle fell down to worship the glorious spirit which he seems to have mistaken for Christ, he told him plainly, "I am of thy fellow servants, the prophets; not God, not an angel, but a human spirit. And in how many ways may they 'minister to the heirs of salvation ?' "

Conscious of and rejoicing in the sweet and holy influences of God's ministering angels, inspired the late Bishop Simpson (Methodist) to say in one of his eloquent sermons : "The very grave itself is a passage into the beautiful and glorious. We have laid our friends in the grave, but they are around us. The little children who sat upon our knee, into whose eyes we look with love, whose little hands have clasped our neck, on whose cheek we have imprinted the kiss—we can almost feel the throbbing of their hearts to-day. They have passed from us, but where are they? Just beyond the line of the visible. And the fathers and mothers who educated us—that directed and comforted us—where are they but just beyond the line of the visible? The associates of our lives, that walk along life's pathway, those with whom we took sweet council, and who dropped from our side—where are they but just beyond us?—not far away, but now it may be very near us. Is there anything to alarm us in this thought? No. It seems to me sometimes that when my head is on the pillow there comes whispers as of joy, which drop into my heart thoughts of the sublime and beautiful and glorious, as though some angel's wing passed over my brow, and some dear one sat by my pillow and communed with my heart to raise my affection toward the other and better world. The invisible is not dark, it is glorious. Sometimes the veil becomes so thin it seems to me I can almost see the bright forms through it, and my bending ear can almost hear the voices of those who are singing their melodious strains. Oh, there is music all around us, though the ear of man hear it not, there are glorious forms all about us, though in the busy scenes of life we recognize them not. The veil of the future will soon be lifted, and the invisible shall appear."

We have shown, dear reader, that the various phases of mediumship as practiced by mediums to-day were possessed and practiced by God's own people in Bible times. The same laws that governed then govern to-day; what was possible then is possible to-day. As to whether spiritualism is true or not, we would say, investigate honestly, casting all prejudice aside and as "the proof of the pudding is in the eating" I have no fear of any one rejecting it who will investigate as I have done. There are frauds everywhere: in the Church, in State, in business and social life, and Spiritualism is no exception.

While writing there lays before me a book entitled "Crimes of Preachers," giving an account of over two thousand crimes of every description under heaven, committed by preachers since 1886, giving the names, crime committed, place of residence, trial and sentence of each. I would not for a moment think of condemning Christianity because of these frauds, neither should we condemn Spiritualism because now and then there are to be found those who would deceive and practice fraud. As there are many who would like to investigate, I have thought best to give here the following rules for investigation, which I copy from "Religion of Spiritualism," by Rev. Samuel Watson, as copied by him from the "London Spiritualist."

HOW TO INVESTIGATE—HOW TO FORM CIRCLES AND DEVELOP MEDIUMSHIP.

"Inquirers into the phenomena of Spiritualism should begin

by forming circles in their own homes, with no spiritualist or professional medium present. Should no results be obtained on the first occasion, try again with other sitters. One or more persons possessing medial powers without knowing it are to be found in nearly every household.

"Let the room be of a comfortable temperature, but cool rather than warm—let arrangements be made that nobody shall enter it and that there shall be no interruption for one hour during the sitting of the circle.

"Let the circle consist of four, five, or six individuals, about the same number of each sex. Sit around an uncovered wooden table, with all the palms of the hands in contact with the top surface. Whether the hands touch each other or not is of usually no importance. Any table will do, just large enough to accommodate the sitters. The removal of a hand from the table for a few seconds does no harm, but when one of the sitters breaks the circle by leaving the table, it sometimes, but not always, considerably delays the manifestations.

"Before the sitting begins, place some pointed lead pencils and some sheets of clean writing-paper on the table to write down any communication that may be obtained.

"People who do not like each other should not sit in the same circle, for such a want of harmony tends to prevent manifestations, except with well-developed physical mediums; it is not yet known why. Belief or unbelief has no influence on the manifestations, but an acrid feeling against them is frequently found to be a weakening influence.

"Before the manifestations begin, it is well to engage in general conversation or in singing, and it is best if neither be of a frivolous nature.

"The first symptoms of the invisible power at work is often a feeling like a cold wind sweeping over the hands. The first manifestations will probably be table-tiltings or raps.

"When motions of the table or sounds are produced freely, to avoid confusion, let one person only speak; he should talk to the table as to an intelligent being. Let him tell the table that three tilts or raps mean 'Yes,' one means 'No,' and two mean 'Doubtful,' and ask whether the arrangement is understood. If three signals be given in answer, then say: If I speak the letters of the alphabet slowly, will you signal every time I come to the letter you want, and spell us out a message? Should three signals be given, set to work on the plan proposed, and from this time an intelligent system of communication is established.

"Afterward the question should be put, 'Are we sitting in the right order to get the best manifestations?' Probably some members of the circle will then be told to change seats with each other and the signals will afterward be strengthened. Next ask, "Who is the medium?' When the intelligence asserts itself to be related or known to anybody present, well chosen questions should be put to test the accuracy of the statements, as the alleged spirits are found to exhibit all the virtues and all the failures of humanity."

"A medium is usually a person of an impulsive, affectionate and genial nature, and very sensitive to mesmeric influences. Mediums are of both sexes.

"The best manifestations are obtained when the medium and all the members of the circle are strongly bound together by the affections, and are thoroughly comfortable and happy. Family circles, with no strangers present, are usually the best.

"Possibly at the first sitting of a circle symptoms of other forms of mediumship than tilts or raps may make their appearance, while by sitting regularly two or three times a week the manifestations will rapidly develop.

"Among the varied phases of phenomena already observed by investigators, may be noted the following : Movement of physical objects, both with and without contact with the sitters; direct writing, drawing, and voices; entrancement, trance and inspirational utterances, temporary materialization, involuntary writing, healing; visions, impressions, as well as many phenomena observed in the study of mesmerism.

"Possibly symptoms of other forms of mediumship, such as trance or clairvoyance, may develop; the better class of messages, as judged by their religious and philosophical merits, usually accompany trance and clairvoyant manifestations, rather than the more objective phenomena. After the manifestations are obtained, the observers should not go to the other extreme, and give way to an excess of credulity, but should believe no more about them or the contents of the messages than they are forced to do by undeniable proof."

We are often asked the question, What do the Spiritualists believe? We would say that there are different shades of belief among those who believe in spirit return, and while it is impossible for spiritualists to have any set form of belief or creed, so long as the truth is progressive, yet we believe that the majority of spiritualists could submit to the following articles, especially those in Christian countries :

1st—We believe in one God, the Soul and Ruler of the Universe, a conscious entity dwelling in the universe, as its master. That God is a law unto himself and that all matter obeys His will through natural law.

2nd—We believe in the Divine mission and work of Christ and that the Christ principle which came from God the Father, and dwelt in Jesus, is to save the world, but that no man can be saved through Christ unless he takes into his life the Christ principle, and that we are saved by what we live, not by what we believe.

3rd—We believe in future rewards and punishments and that the only way to escape the consequences of our wrong-doing is by a genuine heart-felt repentance, followed by the undoing of our wrongs to the best of our ability, and the living out of the Christ principle in our lives, and that "As the tree falleth so shall it lie;" that is, that we enter the spirit-world no better, nor no worse than we leave this world and that we begin life there just where we leave it off here, but that the path of progression is ever open to all of God's children, both here and in the spirit-world, who may have an earnest desire to better their condition, and that all punishment is for correction.

4th—We believe man—all mankind—to be literal sons and daughters of God and the soul of man to be a spark of divinity, and as such it is immortal and undying, and that man, while on the earth plane, is a three-fold being, composed of a material body, the Soul, or Ego, and a Spiritual body, the two latter surviving the former, for which they will never have further use.

5th—We believe that man is sown, at birth into this world, in corruption, but is raised at death,—birth into the spiritual world—in incorruption. That he "is sown in dishonor, raised in glory." "Sown in weakness, raised in power." "Sown a natural body, raised a spiritual body."

6th—We believe that the only veil between this and the spirit-world are these coarse material bodies of ours, and that under favorable conditions the spirits of the so-called dead can come back to earth's children and communicate sweet messages of love to them, and that by the chemical and electrical manipulation of atoms they can mould a material body in a few minutes, which by the ordinary process of nature would require years to produce, and that they can as quickly dematerialize it again.

7th—We believe that heaven and hell are conditions and that the only way to gain heaven in the great hereafter is to have heaven in you while here, and this we believe can only be done by living out the "Christ-life" in our lives. The humble Nazarene once said, "The kingdom of heaven is within you." So we say; that either the kingdom of heaven or of hell is in each of us, and we will carry either the one or the other of those kingdoms with us into the spirit life, and that we make our own heaven or hell the same in the spirit life as we do here.

8th—We believe that the only sanction of the doctrine of eternal punishment to be found in the Bible is in the mistranslation of the Greek word *Aion*, in Matt. 25:46. "And these shall go away into everlasting punishment (Greek, Kolasin Aionion), but the righteous into life eternal." The word Kolasin is derived from *kolazoo*, which in the Greek signifies: 1—To cut off, as lopping off branches of trees; to prune. 2—To restrain, to repress. 3—To chastise, to punish.

That an Aion is a limited time is proven by the fact that it can be made plural, and no multiple of a limited time can be synonymous with eternity. The following are a few of the many passages where the word in its many forms appears, in none of which can it be used in the sense of eternal :

"The children of this world (Aionos) marry and are given in marriage." Luke 20:34.

"But they that shall be counted worthy to obtain that world (Aionos) and the resurrection from the dead, neither marry nor are given in marriage." Luke 20:35.

"And be not conformed to this world." (Aioni). Rom. 12:2.

"Where is the disputers of this world." (Aainos). I Cor. 1:20.

"Howbeit we speak wisdom among them that are perfect: yet not knowing the wisdom of this world (Aionos) nor of the princes of this world (Aionos) that come to nought." I Cor. 2:6.

"Which God ordained before the world (Aionon) unto our glory." I Cor. 2:7.

"Which none of the princes of this world (Aionos) knew." I Cor. 2:8.

"If any among you seem to be wise in this world (Aioni) let him become a fool that he may be wise." I Cor. 3:18.

"In whom the God of this world (Aionos) hath blinded the minds of them which believe not." II Cor. 4:4.

"That he might deliver us from the present evil world." (Aionos). Gal. 1:4.

"Charge them that are rich in this world (Aioni) that they be not high-minded." I Tim. 6:17.

"For Demas hath forsaken me, having loved this present evil world." (Aiona). II Tim, 4:10.

"We should live soberly, righteously and godly, in this present world." (Aioni). Titus 2:12.

"Which God ordained before the world." (Aionon). I Cor. 2:7.

"Not only in this world (Aioni) but in that which is to come." Eph. 1:21.

"The harvest is the end of the world (Aionas) and the reapers are the angels." Matt. 13:39.

"So shall it be in the end of this world." (Aionos). Matt. 13:40.

In the above passages we have the Greek word *Aion* in its various forms, rendered 'world' no less than seventeen times. We might give many more where it has been translated 'age' or 'ages,' as in the following: "That in the ages (Aiosi) to come he might show the exceeding riches of his grace in his kindness toward us through Christ Jesus."—Eph. 2:7. "Even the mystery which hath been hid from ages (Aionon) and from generations, but now is made manifest to his saints."—Col. 1:26.

Words of like meaning may be substituted one for the other without destroying the sense of a passage. Apply this test to any one of the above passages of Scripture, using instead of 'world' or 'ages' the words 'eternal,' 'eternity,' or 'eternities,' and the sense is at once destroyed. If an Aion is a limited time, as the above passages prove, then the punishment of the wicked may be for a limited time. I have given the above because it has always been the teaching of the Church that the event called death changes the attitude of God from that of a kind and loving Father to a cruel, vindictive being, and that no matter how sorry a soul may be for the sins of this life and however much it may desire to rise out of its fallen condition, God's favor is forever withdrawn from that soul after the change called death.

My dear reader, spiritualism knows no such God as this, the God we worship being all love, all goodness, whose love is infinite, extending to all his creatures both here and in the spirit world. In the last quarter of a century the fires of hell have been extinguished so that a hell of "fire and brimstone" has become—as the Rev. Charles H. Fitzwilliam once said in a sermon on Hell—"a back number," and with it that other twin doctrine and blasphemy against the character of a loving Heavenly Father—eternal torment—is doomed to oblivion. That there are spirits in the hells of the spirit world, who have suffered for a long time and who, perhaps, may remain there for ages to come, there is not the shadow of a doubt in the mind of the writer, but it is not because death has changed the attitude of God toward that soul, or that his favor is withdrawn, but because that soul is satisfied to remain in its fallen state and has no desire to better its condition, and as long as a soul prefers hell to heaven even God himself cannot make a heaven for such a soul, and if He, in his loving kindness should, it would to that soul be another hell, because its likes and dislikes are such as to unfit it for the enjoyment of holy companionship, and it would deliberately gravitate to its own place again, where it could surround itself with such companions as are best suited to itself, who have the same likes, dislikes, and evil cravings. And I want to say that if every soul could be brought to understand that as naturally as water finds its own level, so will every spirit on leaving the body gravitate to its own place and be drawn to those who are in every respect as they are, that the thought of the horror of such a soul would stimulate one to a course of right living here.

I am aware that some will say that this picture of hell is rather an orthodox one. Let it be so, the picture has not been overdrawn. Every honest spiritualist knows that this has been the teaching of many spirits, who have been permitted to come back to us and tell of their wretched condition in spirit life, while others again have told us that they have seen their mistakes, and with the earnest desire have progressed away from their former beliefs and lives and are now happy. I would like to say here to those who are now developing, or seeking to develop mediumship, that unless you are living pure lives it were far better that you never became mediums, for as like attracts like, so you must expect to draw to yourselves just such spirits as you yourselves are. What spiritualism needs today is pure mediums, and this applies alike to all spiritualists, whether mediums or not. There are many today who claim to be spiritualists who are anything but spiritual.

For such I have only pity. True spiritualism spiritualizes. Many who are spiritualists in name try to tear down all that is good in Christianity. To me Christianity is a blessed faith, and to take the Christ spirit out of this world, I would want to leave it myself. Do away with the Bible if you will; close up the churches, let all the best minds in the world come together and establish a code of morals for the government of men, and that code of morals would be nothing more or less than Christianity in its broadest sense. Christianity, *if lived out*, cannot be improved upon. If every one in this world of ours was a good, pure, genuine, whole-souled Christian we would need no locks, bolts or bars, and this world of ours would be transformed into a heaven, for then every man would acknowledge every other man as his brother and God as father of us all. That person who *lives* the Christ-life is a truly happy person here and his happiness in the hereafter is assured.

The following is a partial list of eminent persons who have investigated the phenomena generally known as psychical, or spiritualistic, and have become convinced of the truth of spirit return :

SCIENTISTS.

Alfred R. Wallace, the Discoverer of Evolution.
Dr. Lockart Robertson, Editor Journal of Medical Science.
Cromwell Varley, Electrician, F. R. S., C. E.
Dr. William Gregory, F. R. S. E.
Herman Goldsmith, Astronomer and Physicist.
W. F. Barrett, F. R. E., Professor of Physics in the Royal College of Science, Dublin.
Dr. Ashburner.
Dr. U. Hitchman, Physiologist and Physicist.
Wm. Crookes, Chemist.
Alex Von Humboldt.
Prof. N. D. Wagner, Geologist, University of St. Petersburg.
Prof. A. Butlerov, Chemist, University of St. Petersburg.
Dr. Hoeffle, Author of Historical Chemistry.
Prof. Nees Von Esenbeck, Prest. Royal Academy of Sciences, Breslau, Germany.
Dr. J. Elliottson, F. R. S., some time Prest. of the Royal Med. and Chir. Soc., London.
Camille Flammarion, Astronomer.
Prof. De Morgan, Prest. Math. Soc., London.
Prof. William Denton, Geologist.
Dr. Vladimer Dahl of St. Petersburg Academy of Science.
Dr. Herbert Mayo, F. R. S.
Prof. F. Zollner of Leipsic, author of Transcendental Physics.
Prof. Worthen, State Geologist of Illinois.
Dr. Maximillian Perty, Prof. Nat. Science., Berne, Switzerland.
Prof. Robert Hare, Chemist.
Prof. J. J. Mapes, Agricultural Chemist.

Prof. W. D. Gunning, Geologist.
Prof. J. R. Buchanan, Anthropologist.
Baron von Reichenbach, Physiologist.
The Earl of Crawford and Balcarres, F. R. S., Prest. R. A. S.

PHYSICIANS.

Dr. Jos. Haddock, England
Dr. J. J. Groth Wilkinson
Dr. J. M. Gully
Dr. Stanhope Templeman,
  Speer, Edinburg.

Dr. Julius Frauenstadt, Germ'ny
Dr. Grunhut, Buda-Pesth
Dr. Gray Sexton, London
Dr. G. W. Langedor, Mannheim
Dr. J. M. Peebles

PHILOSOPHERS AND METAPHYSICIANS.

Prof. S. B. Brittan, Moral and Mental Philosophy.
P. Yowkevitsch, Prof. Phil., University of St. Petersburg.
A. Bronson Alcott.
J. H. von Fichte, the Emerson of Germany.
Dr. Franz Hoffman, Prof. Phil., Wurtzburg, Germany.
Dr. Robert Freise, Breslau.
Narson E. Senior, Prof. of Political Economy, Oxford, England.
Prof. W. E. Weber of Cottingen.
Prof. G. F. Fechner.

EMINENT STATESMEN AND PHILANTHROPISTS.

Ex-Gov. A. P. Tallmage of Wisconsin.
Ex-Vice President B. F. Wade
Hon. Joshua R. Giddings of Ohio.
Abraham Lincoln
Ex-Vice President Henry Wilson.
Victor Hugo
Ex-President Andrew Johnson
George Thompson
Guisippi Garibaldi
Louis Kossuth
William Lloyd Garrison
Senator Sprague, of R. I.

M. Francois Guizot, author and Statesman.
Leon Favre, Consul General of France.
Jules Favre, his brother
Senator Fitch, of Indiana
Senator Harris, of Louisiana
Senator Stewart, of Nevada
Hon. Robert Dale Owen, Late Foreign Minister
Hon. N. P. Banks, of Mass.
Senator Howard, of Michigan
Hon. G. W. Julian, of Indiana
Senator Simons, of R. I.
Senator Anthony, of R. I.

DISTINGUISHED LITERARY AND ARTISTIC CELEBRITIES.

Trowbridge, the Artist
Florence Marryatt
Wm. and Mary Howitt

Mr. and Mrs. S. C. Hall
T. Adolphus Trollopp, the popular Novelist.

Gerald Massey, the Poet
W. M. Thackeray
Sir Edward Lytton and Son
Epes Sargent
Mark M. (Brick) Pomeroy

Hiram Powers, famous Sculptor
Robert Chambers
Mrs. Eliz'b'th Barrett Browning
Captain R. F. Burton, African
Traveler and Author
Hamlin Garland, Literary.

CROWNED HEADS, NOBILITY, ETC.

Queen Victoria, of England
Emperor Alexander, of Russia
Emp'r Louis Napoleon, France
Prince Wittgenstein, Lt. Gen.,
Aid-de-camp to Emperor of
Russia
Hon. Alexander Askakoff, Russian Imperial Councilor, St.
Petersburg, Russia.
Baron von Dirkinck, of Holmfeld Holstein
Le Compte de Bullett, of Paris
Lord Lindsay
Lord Adare
Lord Lyndhurst
Duke of Leuchtenburg, Germ'y
Hon. A. B. Richmond, Meadville, Pa.
Hon. W. J. Bryan, of Nebraska

Sir W. Travelyn
Countess Caithness
Sir T. Willshire
Lady Cowper
Sir Charles Isham, Bart
Sir Charles Napier
Bishop Clark, of R. I.
Col. E. B. Wilbraham, of the
English Army.
Judge Dailey, Brooklyn, N. Y.
Judge J. W. Edmunds
Judge Ladd
Judge Lawrence
Sergeant E. W. Cox ⎫
H. D. Jenckens ⎪
H. D. Durphy   ⎬
Lord Dunraven ⎭
English Barristers
Hon. A. B. French, Clyde, O.

Hon. L. V. Moulton, Grand Rapids, Mich.

TESTIMONY OF EMINENT MEN.

Lord Brougham—"Even in the most cloudless skies of skepticism I see a rain-cloud, if it be no bigger than a man's hand: it is Modern Spiritualism."

Camille Flammarion—"I do not hesitate to affirm my conviction, based on personal examination of the subject, that any scientific man who declares the phenomena, denominated 'magnetic,' 'somnambulic,' 'mediumistic,' and others not yet explained by science, to be 'impossible,' is one who speaks without knowing what he is talking about."

A. R. Wallace—"We are justified in taking the facts of Modern Spiritualism (and with them the spiritual theory as the only tenable one) as being fully established. Its whole course and history proclaimed it to be neither imposture nor delusion, nor surval of the beliefs of savages, but a great and all-important truth."

The London Dialectical Committee report—"That sounds of a varied character, apparently proceeding from articles of furniture, the floor, and walls, occur without being produced by muscular action or mechanical contrivance, or adequate exertion of muscular force by those present, and frequently without contact of any person. That these sounds and movements often occur in the manner asked for by some person present, and * * * * answer questions, and spell out coherent communications."

J. H. Fichte, the German Philosopher and Author—"I feel it my duty to bear testimony to the great fact of Spiritualism. No one should keep silent."

Prof. De Morgan, Late President of the Mathematical Society of London—"I have both seen and heard, in a manner that should make unbelief impossible, things called spiritual, which cannot be taken by a rational being to be capable of explanation by imposture, coincidence, or mistake."

Dr. Robert Chambers—"I have for many years known that these phenomena are real."

Prof. Challis, the late Plumerian Prof. of Astronomy at Cambridge—"I have been unable to resist the large amount of testimony to such facts, which has come from many independent sources, and from a vast number of witnesses. * * * In short, the testimony has been so abundant and consentaneous, that either the facts must be admitted to be such as are reported, or the possibility of certifying facts by human testimony must be given up."—*Clerical Journal, June, 1862.*

Prof. Hare, Professor of Chemistry in the University of Pa.—"Far from abating my confidence in the inferences respecting the agencies of the spirits of deceased mortals, in the manifestations of which I have given in my work, I have had even more striking evidences of that agency than those given in the work in question."

William Crookes, F. R. S., etc.—"That a hitherto unrecognized form of Force—whether it be called physical or psychical is of little consequence—is involved in this occurrence is not with me a matter of opinion, but of absolute knowledge."

Professors Tornebom and Edland, the Swedish Physicists—"Only those deny the realty of spiritual phenomena who have never examined them; but profound study alone can explain them."

Baron Carl DuPrel (Munich)—"This intelligence can read, write and understand the language of human beings, frequently such as is unknown to the medium. It is no use whatever to fight against this proposition."

Dr. Lochkart Robertson—"The writer can no more doubt the physical manifestations of so-called Spiritualism than he would any other fact."

William Howitt—"Spiritualism having reached its millions of adherents, is now beyond the influence of opponents."

Thackeray—"It is all very well for you, who have probably never seen any spiritual manifestations, to talk as you do; but had you seen what I have seen, you would hold a different opinion."

Rev. M. J. Savage—"That he is in possession of a respectable body of facts that he does not know how to explain, except on the theory that he is dealing with some invisible intelligence."

Prof. Elliott Coues—"In full view, a few inches from my face, I distinctly saw the pencil write 'of itself;' and finish the last word or two of a sentence which straggled over most of the slate. That I saw it, just as described, is simply true."

Judge A. H. Dailey, of Brooklyn, N. Y—"I have seen independent slate-writing. Mr. Kellar and Mr. Herrmann, the magicians, many criticise this phenomena as they see fit, but I undertake to say that it is absolutely impossible for them to imitate it, or produce anything like it under the same conditions. If they will come here and allow me to take my own slates and put them down on that table, one on top of the other, a piece of slate-pencil between the two, the slates held together with my hand on top—if they will write on those slates while I am holding them there I will give them $1000. But they must not touch them. I have seen slate writing done under such conditions. Once the writing was over the name of my father, and another time over the signature of a deceased sister of my wife's. There were two separate hand writings. My father had been dead for about thirty years and died a long distance from where this phenomenon presented itself. My wife's sister had been dead about fifteen years, and it was utterly impossible for the medium in this case to have known the name of either. Then I have seen a hand produced in broad sunlight without the aid of a cabinet, in a room containing five windows, the blinds being open. On that occasion I was sitting at the table with two other persons. I have seen a naked hand without an arm to it produced before me. In the presence of five persons I have seen unexpectedly, right close by my side, without any cabinet or any preparation, or any idea that there was going to be anything like the phenomenon presented while we were sitting at a table. I have seen the form of human beings slowly shape itself from a sort of etherized substance of lightish color until it took on the form of a person, with a body, limbs and head, finally disappearing with the rapidity of lightning. I have seen that done five times, once in the evening when the light was sufficiently bright to read the newspaper. Spiritualists claim, and I think with good reason, that if you take everything that we denominate the phenomena of spiritualism out of the Bible it would cease to be a religious book."—*From Philadelphia Press, Sunday, July 30th, 1893.*

Forty years ago the first spirit raps were heard in the home of the Fox family at Hydesville N. Y. Since that time the growth of modern Spiritualism has been phenomenal, considering the opposition it has had to contend against. Scientists treated it with bitter contempt. Learned doctors tried to expose it; D.D's condemned it; not many of the learned and wise believed in it but, like all other great truths, it has found its way into the hearts of those who were not too proud to accept it, clad as it was in the garb of an outcast. Since then it has spread throughout the whole world, until it has ramified all classes of society. "From peasant cots to kingly thrones, from beggars to millionairs, and from lowly artisans to kings, queens and emperors, extends an unbroken chain of believers in this philosophy, this faith, this religion of Spiritualism." Many are enemies to spiritualism because they are ignorant as to its strength and standing and know nothing as to its teachings. There are, as before stated, about ten million Spiritualists in the United States, maintaining between forty and fifty camp-grounds where camp-meetings are held at some time during the year, the attendance in many cases running up into the thousands. The following is a partial list only of the camps:

Haslet Park Camp, Mich., has eighteen acres of land and thirty cottages are built.

Vicksburg Camp, Mich., occupies a beutiful grove of forty acres. The association has a fine auditorium, a hotel, cottages and lodging-house.

Onset Bay Mass., has a temple that will seat 1,500 people. There are 500 cottages on the camp proper. Has been organized 18 years. At Harwich, Mass., is another camp which has existed for twenty-seven years, holding successful meetings.

De Leon Springs Camp, Florida, is a winter camp where good meetings are held.

In California, Summerland Camp is regularly organized, and many others are held in different places in the State.

Parkland Camp, Pa., contains 150 acres, with a number of fine cottages, hotel, restaurant, pavilion, etc.

Temple Heights Camp, Maine, has some thirty cottages on the ground.

Sunapee Camp, N. H., is located at Sunapee Lake.

At Lake Pleasant Camp, Mass., there are about 400 cottages built, and more contemplated.

Clinton Camp, Iowa, owns 19 acres of land and has a pavilion seating about 1800 people. A number of cottages are built.

Vernon Park Camp, Maine, has thirty cottages, good boarding-houses, and a fine pavilion for holding meetings in.

Merimac Island Camp is near St. Paul, Minn., and has a good attendance.

Delphos Camp, Kansas, besides its present location, owns the most beautiful natural oak grove in the State.

Lily Dale Camp, at Cassadaga, N. Y. has 46 acres of ground, over 150 cottages, a grand hotel, stores, a large auditorium, and its fine water works and flower-gemmed parks make it "a thing of joy forever."

Queen City Park, Burlington, Vt., has twenty acres of ground.

Mountain Lake Park, Md., has 800 acres of ground; the park is lighted by electricity.

Lookout Mountain Camp, Tenn., is a fine, large camp, surrounded by the most beautiful natural scenery.

Magnolia Camp, Pensacola Bay, Florida, is a new camp containing some twenty acres of ground. Is most beautifully situated. Has a large 50 room hotel, and about twenty cottages are to be erected.

The following are a few of the many camps which it is impossible to describe here: Cherry Vale Camp, Kan.; Lake Harbor, Mich.; Chesterfield, Ind.; Lake George Camp, N. Y.; Maumee Valley, Ohio; Devils Lake, Mich.; Catalpa Park, N. Y.; Maple Dell, Ohio; Lake Brady, Ohio; Mantua Station, Ohio; Woolley Park, Ashley, Ohio; Verona, Maine; Niantic, Conn., Etna, Maine; New Era, Ore.; Cape Cod, Mass.; Echo Grove, Lynn, Mass.; Twin City Park, Minn.; Muskegon, Mich.; Lake Helen, Florida; Haslett Park, Mich.; Orion, Mich.; Montpelier, Ind.; Como Park, Minn.; Liberal, Mo.; Denver, Col.

Besides the above there are scores of grove meetings being

held every year in the different states, which will eventually result in the organization of new camps. Spiritualistic temples are also being erected all over the United States, where services are held regularly.

Now dear reader, whatever may have been your belief in regard to Spiritualism, I think you will be convinced by this time that the phenomena of Spiritualism and its phases of mediumship have some foundation in the Bible. And now, little book, I send you forth, hoping that you may lead some out of the bondage of prejudice and superstition into the light of spiritual freedom and liberty.

LEWIS L. EVARTS.

137 S. Market St., Shamokin, Pa.